£3

TRUTH
ALWAYS PREVAILS

SADRUDDIN HASHWANI

TRUTH
ALWAYS PREVAILS

A Memoir

PORTFOLIO
PENGUIN

PORTFOLIO

Published by the Penguin Group

Penguin Books India Pvt. Ltd, 7th Floor, Infinity Tower C, DLF Cyber City, Gurgaon 122 002, Haryana, India

Penguin Group (USA) Inc., 375 Hudson Street, New York, New York 10014, USA

Penguin Group (Canada), 90 Eglinton Avenue East, Suite 700, Toronto, Ontario, M4P 2Y3, Canada

Penguin Books Ltd, 80 Strand, London WC2R 0RL, England

Penguin Ireland, 25 St Stephen's Green, Dublin 2, Ireland (a division of Penguin Books Ltd)

Penguin Group (Australia), 707 Collins Street, Melbourne, Victoria 3008, Australia

Penguin Group (NZ), 67 Apollo Drive, Rosedale, Auckland 0632, New Zealand

Penguin Books (South Africa) (Pty) Ltd, Block D, Rosebank Office Park, 181 Jan Smuts Avenue, Parktown North, Johannesburg 2193, South Africa

Penguin Books Ltd, Registered Offices: 80 Strand, London WC2R 0RL, England

First published in Portfolio by Penguin Books India 2014

ISBN 9780670085224

Typeset in Bembo Std by Eleven Arts, Delhi
Printed at Replika Press Pvt. Ltd, India

A PENGUIN RANDOM HOUSE COMPANY

To my loving parents,
Zaverbai and Hussain Hashwani

CONTENTS

Contents

INTRODUCTION

Who am I and why am I writing this book? I am writing this book with the same optimism and hope with which I have lived my life, through all that my friends and foes and the positive and negative energies of this world have thrown at me. That is why I must begin with dedicating my book to the youth of Pakistan and to the young men and women of my country as well as of the larger region of south and central Asia, at the crossroads of which sits Pakistan. I pray my book can enlighten them. I pray my book can help them. Above all, I hope my book can inspire them to build a better Pakistan and a better tomorrow—a just, fair and prosperous society that the 200 million people of our country deserve.

A memoir is meant to be a celebration of life and achievement. However, I intend to make my book not a paean to myself but a thanksgiving to my country, my people and that great God, Allah as we address him, who has given me more than I deserved and wished for. Even so, life could have and should have been easier if the circumstances of Pakistan and the intentions of those who have ruled it for so many years had always been honourable. Sadly, this has often not been the case. As such, my book is not just about my achievements and corporate balance sheets—it is as much the story of a businessman who struggled against corrupt politicians and dictators to nurture an enterprise.

Enterprise is the enemy of dictatorship. Enterprise demands transparency, creates jobs and triggers opportunities. Transparency and opportunities are not what politicians and dictators want in the public sphere. Rather than give young people jobs, they want to exploit young people for their own ends, often through emotive causes. It is almost as if they have a vested interest in poverty—or so my experience tells me. Alas, this has also been the experience of Pakistan over the past six decades.

I am a proud Muslim and a proud Pakistani. My family has lived in Pakistan for seven generations. My adult, conscious life has straddled the history of Pakistan as a free nation. I am a product of its ebbs and flows, its peaks and troughs, its cricket triumphs and economic slumps, its tender hopes and innocent dreams, its innermost fears and terrifying nightmares. I am nothing if not a Pakistani. I know this country and its history not merely because I was born into it or love it but because I have grown up and grown old with it.

Pakistan was carved out as an independent nation in 1947. It had golden aspirations. It was rich in human resources and blessed with agricultural plenty. It had an industrial base and mineral resources. It had an excellent port in Karachi, one of the best in post-War Asia. It also had a population determined to make things work and to build a happy nation where all citizens, rich and poor and regardless of background, could live together.

This dream has only partially been realized. Today, Pakistan faces a huge public relations challenge and is known for violence and instability, for chronic corruption and joblessness, for power cuts and economic meltdowns. Why? To be sure, as a nation, Pakistan has been drained by wars that it did not start and did not want. The crisis in neighbouring Afghanistan has taken its toll on Pakistan for forty years now. Through successive wars and invasions— by the Soviet Union in 1979 and by the Americans and their allies in 2001—Pakistan has been a staging ground for conflict. In terms of resources, economic viability and human lives, it has suffered greatly.

Whether it was dealing with a monumental refugee burden or losing hundreds and thousands of people to bullets and bombs, enemy soldiers and terrorist attacks, it is Pakistan that has suffered more than any other country. For the superpowers of the world, the Afghan War of 1979–89 and the battles that began in 2001 were elaborate games of chess or, if I could be permitted to mix metaphors, a distant conflict being played out on a screen, almost like a video or computer game. For Pakistan, these wars and battles have been physically and emotionally draining. They have sucked out the vitality of two generations of our people. As a result of all this, Pakistan has come to make international headlines in a manner that no true Pakistani or true follower of Islam would want.

How did we come to this pass and how can we get out of it? In this book, I have raised these questions and searched for answers, using the prism of my life and career. I must confess I am not an intellectual; I have not learnt about the world through books and doctoral theses. My learning has been experiential. I have slept in the backs of trucks in the cold deserts of Balochistan and I have also slept in plush five-star hotel rooms. It is my privilege that I have learnt from both, that I have never stopped learning. Indeed, if you follow the teachings of Prophet Muhammad, Peace Be Upon Him, and practise detachment from material comforts and focus only on the enrichment of the soul, then it doesn't really matter whether you sleep under the sky, with the desert sand blowing into your face, or on a soft mattress in an air-conditioned suite.

I am not writing this book to tell you how I made it from the desert to a hotel suite, from fairly humble, middle-class origins to a state where, by the grace of Allah, I have enough. That is scarcely something to be proud of or to write about. It is almost inconsequential. I will try and explain why. I am associated with many companies and entities but the one that gives me the greatest satisfaction is the Hashoo Foundation, of which my daughter is the chairperson. The foundation has worked in areas as diverse as education and public health, dairy development and honeybee farming, and has even put in place a successful skill development project for Afghan refugees in Pakistan. It has helped about half a million people in their fight against poverty and in their quest for better lives.

I am not flattered by the achievements of the Hashoo Foundation. Indeed, I am thankful for the privilege that the Almighty has accorded me to help my fellow human beings and my Pakistani brothers and sisters. This work is not for publicity and, despite the urgings of friends, I will not write on the Hashoo Foundation and its philanthropic interventions in this book. That is not my purpose. This work is for inner peace and a deeper satisfaction; it is an answer to and a salutation to Allah. In the same manner,

I must add, my professional career and the companies and businesses I have set up and run give me satisfaction because, at the end of the day, they help people: they create jobs, nurture local economies and raise living standards for ordinary people on the margins of the hotels or factories that the Hashoo Group promotes. For me, this is the ultimate mandate of business. It is the essence of capitalism. It is also, and this may surprise my non-Muslim readers, the essence of Islam.

I never had the advantage of attending a fancy management school to get a high degree in business administration. My management techniques and business practices are self-learnt. If anything, they are inspired by the Quran—a repository of wisdom that I find myself turning to very often and one that leaves me calmer and intellectually wealthier each time I read it—and by Islam as I have been taught to love and cherish it. For all the misconceptions about it, especially in the West, it is actually a very easy-going and liberating faith. It demands very little of those who practise it, and calls for egalitarianism and equality, for justice and fairness, before that One God. In a sense, that is the only message of Islam—a simple and beautiful message. That is what makes Islam a very practical religion and a way of life that is easy to adapt to.

It is not without reason that the Prophet was a householder, combining spiritual wisdom with everyday insights from his life as a merchant and trader. He was descended from the venerable Hashim, his great-grandfather, who pioneered mercantile trade in Mecca. This aspect of the Prophet's life has never ceased to amaze and move me. In my small way, I have attempted to follow in his footsteps. For me, the exciting phenomenon of building companies and creating wealth for my colleagues, partners and employees has been as much a temporal undertaking as a spiritual one. It has been a corollary to my service to Islam and to my duties as a Muslim.

Islam has taught me to see business as a social calling, not as an end in itself. Many of my business decisions have been based on wagers on the future of Pakistan rather than on calculations of immediate profit. I have taken audacious risks and done so when I believed that Pakistan would benefit if my venture succeeded. This is not a vain and empty boast. From building a hotel in Gwadar—in a desolate township, without any customers—to drilling for oil and exploring gas with the idea of securing energy security for Pakistan, my country and my co-citizens have remained central to my business plans. As I once told an American friend, Pakistan is not just the name on my passport—it is my passion. It has remained a passion even though I have been forced to spend five years outside my beloved country, in virtual exile in Dubai. It has remained a passion even though, close to a dozen times, I have been put on the dreaded and infamous Exit Control List, which prevents the Pakistanis on the list from leaving the country. It has been such a passion that I am perhaps the only Pakistani who was put on the Exit Control List while abroad but rather than stay on overseas, chose to return home and suffer the consequences.

In the world outside, I see myself as Pakistan's spokesperson, defender and self-appointed ambassador. I have stood up for the army and the security establishment in the country in the past decade, while it has been attacked—unfairly I think—by the Western media. In 1998, after India provocatively exploded a nuclear bomb, I was clear in my mind that Pakistan had to respond with its own nuclear tests. True, economic sanctions would follow and my business would suffer too—but that didn't stop me from vociferously insisting that Pakistan's nuclear tests were essential. My personal gains or losses were irrelevant. Pakistan and its security came first.

My problem is that I am too outspoken. I speak my mind more readily than a diplomat would advise. I speak without fear and rancour and I speak quite strongly and openly. This is not always appreciated and has invited hostility from powerful people—business rivals, at times, especially established tycoons who looked upon me as an importunate upstart in my younger days; self-important civil servants; powerful and egotistical dictators and politicians. There are people here who have been trusted with the destiny of Pakistan by its people, but who have betrayed that trust. That they have hurt me is only a side story—the damage they have done to Pakistan is incalculable.

I bear no grudges. As my granddaughter tells me, I lose my temper quickly but cool down as quickly. I go to sleep at night peacefully and carry nothing of a day's quarrels or disagreements to the following morning. These are lessons I learnt early in life from my parents and they have served me well in personal and professional dealings. If somebody stabs me in the back or tries to run me down, I leave it to Allah to protect me and redress it in his own way.

Nevertheless, I do find it difficult to forgive or forget the betrayal of Pakistan. A fundamental teaching of Islam is that we all go empty-handed to the grave. It was a line I first heard when I was a small child and it has stayed with me. In saying this, the Prophet outlined the great philosophy of Islam: surrender to God and practise detachment from greed and material excesses. Sadly, Pakistan's billionaire politicians have forgotten this profound verity, ironically in a nation founded in the glorious name of Islam.

Nations and societies are built by their middle classes and working classes, striving honestly, day after day, to make a better life. In Pakistan, that movement, that churning, has simply not been allowed. Socially and economically,

Pakistan remains a pyramid: the few at the top oppress the many at the bottom. The media talks of the 'Establishment' and the 'forty families' who dominate the country. This is shorthand for an acceptance that new prosperity and the expansion of the middle class—small and medium business enterprises, first-generation white-collar workers, people with higher and technical educational capacities—is systematically sabotaged. Islam is an egalitarian faith and Pakistan was founded on the notion of equality for all. In practice, we have failed our founder, Quaid-e-Azam Muhammad Ali Jinnah, and built a very unequal society with very sharp differentials.

This process—or rather this stagnation—makes me angry and impatient. That anger and that impatience have been the principal motivations for this book. Why do I feel so strongly and emotionally about the lack of opportunities for young, ambitious people in Pakistan? For one, having travelled the world, I recognize that few countries have the sort of potential that Pakistan does. To waste its potential is not just a tragedy, it is a crime. Second, I am a self-made man. I have not descended from a feudal family that owned vast tracts of land for centuries. I grew up in a simple home and inherited no massive property or capital or company. I built things on my own, with labour and luck, with the help of friends and with the blessings of Allah. It has not been easy but it could have been smoother if our rulers had allowed Pakistan a fair and open system of governance. That is what I seek to advocate through this book.

To be a businessman in Pakistan is to negotiate a minefield. Corruption and nepotism are second nature to our politicians and civil servants and, regrettably, to a few senior generals too. They crush and throttle new ideas or initiatives. The system of controls and regulations that has been engineered by our governing elite is designed to protect privilege and not encourage talent or daring. There is corruption in other countries as well but this level of victimization is rare. Others have compromised with the circumstances and given in—I have not and that is why I find myself in Dubai rather than in my treasured Karachi or in my home in Islamabad. It has been gut-wrenching to tear oneself away from the land of one's birth and memories and dreams. Repeated terror attacks on my hotels, an assault on my house, attempts to kidnap my children and threats that forced me to hurriedly transfer them to schools abroad—I would not wish this on an enemy. It was not the life I wanted for myself, and not the rosy future Pakistanis wished for when I was growing up, in the early years of freedom.

As it happens, if my most determined adversaries are to be found in Pakistan, so are my greatest well-wishers. I have helped create employment opportunities and chaperoned entire rural communities into a better future by making them part of my business plans, as ancillary beneficiaries and social partners of the Hashoo Group. It is these countless people, these hidden hands, people whom I don't know, who have prayed for me and whose blessings have kept me going, despite the obstacles stubborn men have placed in my way. These are not empty words—they are emotionally felt and they come straight from the heart. They are also rooted in truth. There is empirical evidence to suggest that no other Pakistani businessman has been harassed non-stop, by successive governments of various persuasions, as I have. I have learnt to shrug my shoulders but, I must confess, it does hurt at times.

As you are aware, I run Pakistan's largest hotel chain that offers world-class hospitality and service, even if I say so myself. One would think this sector and tourism in general would be encouraged by the government, especially since it brings in precious hard currency in the form of dollars and euros. This would, in fact, seem clear as day but policymakers in Pakistan have chosen to be deliberately ignorant. As a result, hotel tariffs in Pakistan are among the lowest in the world but the hotel taxes are extraordinarily high. Those who decide on these taxes are too busy scoring points or mouthing populist slogans to bother with long-term gains for Pakistan. Tourism is an industry that generates several jobs down the line, in a series of related businesses. So many countries have learnt this but not the rulers of Pakistan.

Even if hotel taxes are exorbitantly high, our hotel chain pays them—and pays them honestly. Many other chains don't—they avoid taxes, they under-invoice, they cheat and bribe their way. That is not my credo. No wonder some of my colleagues and executives tell me, and only half-jokingly, that the more inexplicable fiscal and government policies seem to be shaped and framed with the Hashoo Group particularly in mind. I respond with silence, only raising my hands and looking skyward. God knows the truth.

I don't intend to turn this book into a rant against specific individuals. I have been honest and have named names. If some people take it personally, I will have to live with it. My intention is not to target people but to emphasize how things are in Pakistan and how they can and must be changed. This book is also a message—consider it a gift from an experienced man—to the future generations of Pakistan so that they can learn from the mistakes of previous generations and not allow a system to persist if it extracts a price from an honest man who just wants to live honestly.

I have faith in the young people of Pakistan. Their skills, cerebral qualities and willingness to work hard are on par with those of the best on our planet. It is they who must and will build a new Pakistan that will be a world leader in the coming decades. If my book can help them even a little, I will be honoured. With this, I surrender my words and my life story to you.

PROLOGUE

The Children of Fatima

How do I begin? I wrestled long and hard with this question.

Where do I start? I was born in 1940, seven years before the birth of Pakistan, an iconic event that shaped one of my earliest memories and thinking of which still gives me goosebumps. The troubled mid-1940s, the Second World War, insofar that it affected me and my little world, the Muslim–Hindu conflict that led to the partition of British India in August 1947 and the creation of Pakistan, flowing almost seamlessly into the euphoria and optimism of a vibrant new nation in the 1950s—all of these have helped sculpt me and my sensibilities. Yet, if I have to

1

introduce myself to my reader, I need to go back deeper and further to explore the roots of my identity—or rather, my multiple identities.

I was a child of my parents and am now a father and grandfather. Each of those words conveys a different meaning, a different relationship, a different identity. I run a business conglomerate; I carry a dozen cards in my wallet— bank cards, credit cards, a driving licence, cards linking me with various professional and social organizations. Each of these too conveys a different meaning. At the simplest, most basic level—and at the level that matters, actually—I am a Muslim and a Pakistani: no more, no less. For me, that is identity enough. Yet, if I have to tell you of the source code of my identity—in terms of heritage and family history— that answer needs to be qualified or expanded upon.

The Hashwani family are Muslims who form part of a Shia community called the Ismailis. The Ismailis are one of the seventy-two communities of Islam and form an aspect of the rich theological, cultural and ethnic diversity of our shared religion. Of course, the fundamental tenets of Islam define each and every one of these sects. The foundation of Islam is that the Holy Prophet, Mohammad, Peace Be Upon Him, is the Seal of the Prophets and the last of the Prophets God sent to Earth. The Quran is the holy book to all Muslims, irrespective of which sect or society they belong to, and anybody who recites the *kalimah*—'There is no God but Allah and Mohammad is the messenger of Allah'—is accepted as a Muslim. These foundational tenets are unchallenged but, as Islam grows and evolves, so does its diversity. At the time of the Prophet, there were no different sects of Muslims. The four Caliphs who followed the Prophet, played a key role in establishing Islam and leaving the stamp of those early years on the faith that is still with us and which the devout believe will be with us till the end of time.

Among the central and most influential figures in the first years of Islam was Fatima (R.A.), the daughter of the Prophet. She is an intensely revered figure in Islamic history; to this day, 'Fatima' is a popular name for girls born into Muslim households. One of the Prophet's closest followers was his cousin Ali (A.S.), who was like a brother to him. Ali was born in the Kaaba shrine in Mecca and became the first male to accompany the Prophet into the faith of Islam. To Shias, Hazrat Ali (A.S.) was the first Imam, followed by his sons—and the Prophet's grandsons—Hassan (R.A.) and Hussain (R.A.). This was the Ahl al-Bayt—'People of the House' in Arabic—the family of the Prophet. With the passing away of all the sons of the Prophet, the legacy of the family continued through Fatima (R.A.) and her children. The Ahl al-Bayt did much to spread the faith of Islam. Many *auliya*s and preachers owing their origins to this family travelled across the globe to transmit the essence of the Quran and the teachings of the Prophet. That is how Islam moved far from its Arab homeland and became a rich, worldwide faith, with practitioners in China and Russia, throughout Central Asia, Iran and South Asia, even Indonesia and the Philippines besides, of course, Africa and parts of Europe. Ismailis are fortunate to have the blessings and the guidance of the Ahl al-Bayt to this day. Our spiritual leader is His Highness the Aga Khan, the 49th Imam, a direct descendant of Hazrat Ali and the Prophet.

The Ismailis have a rich tradition. They contributed immensely to learning and piety and are known for their charitable and philanthropic concerns as well as their support to social and cultural causes and the alleviation of poverty. When the Ismaili Imams ruled Egypt and established one of the first empires of Islam, they founded the city that we today know as Cairo. About a thousand years ago, Imam al-Moezz, the 14th Imam, founded the Al-Azhar Mosque and the Al-Azhar University, which are among the most important institutions in the Muslim world. It is to be noted that the names of the mosque and the university were derived from Al-Zahra (the 'Luminous' or the 'Brilliant'), a title given to Fatima (R.A.). Imam al-Moezz was later buried in the premises of the Al-Azhar Mosque.

To the believer, the Quran is a complete code of life and a guide at every step. The Ismaili tradition of Imams and pirs played a stellar role in expanding the family of Islam and bringing new converts and adherents into its fold. The Quran was blessed in Arabic but, thanks to wise and far-seeing men, its philosophy was rendered into several languages. An example I can cite is that of Nasir Khusraw, an eleventh-century renaissance man from the Iranian province of Khorasan and a great Ismaili theologian and polymath. A millennium ago, Khusraw travelled to several countries and cities in north Africa and West, Central and South Asia, finally bringing the true message of Islam to the heartland of what is today Pakistan and to its great urban centres like Lahore. In those formative years, Islamic preachers and travellers spread not just the word of Allah but also triggered cultural and economic interaction. That is why Islam became such a compelling part of the landscape of the regions it went to. In their own way, the prominent Ismaili teachers came to exemplify this phenomenon. In Pakistan, for instance, Islam was spread in a variety of local languages: Sindhi, Punjabi, Seraiki, Balochi, and so on. In this form, Islam came to be localized and yet it always remained a universal creed, with the same defining principles. All Muslims, irrespective of the language they speak or the food they eat, acknowledge the Oneness of God, seek the mercy and blessings of Allah and submit to the Last Prophet, Peace Be Upon Him.

How did the Hashwanis, who were originally from Iran, come to settle in Pakistan? In the 1840s, the 46th Imam, Imam Hasan Ali Shah, the first to use the title of His Highness the Aga Khan and known as Aga Khan I, had political differences with the royal family of Iran (then Persia). With his followers, he began a long and hazardous journey that took him from Iran to Afghanistan, then Balochistan, before finally entering British India and Sindh. From Sindh, he travelled to what is now the Indian state of Gujarat and finally reached the metropolis of Bombay in 1845. Due to protests by the Iranian government, the British appealed to the Aga Khan to live for a year in Calcutta, before he returned to Bombay and set up homes there and in the nearby city of Poona. The route that the Aga Khan followed from Iran to Bombay is notable. While he was attacked by brigands and rapacious local warlords on the way, by and large he was welcomed by people of all communities, including fellow Ismailis—all these areas had pre-existing small or substantial Ismaili communities—and by non-Muslim kings such as the ruler of Kutch (now in Gujarat, bordering Pakistan), who had high regard for the Aga Khan and the Ismailis. Aga Khan I was the great-great-grandfather of the current leader of the Ismaili community, His Highness Prince Karim Aga Khan or Aga Khan IV, the 49th Imam.

Among those who travelled as part of Imam Hasan Ali Shah's caravan from Iran to British India was Mukhi

Tharoo, my great-great-grandfather. As the Ismaili community entered South Asia under the leadership of the 46th Imam, members of the entourage settled down along the way. That is how an impressive Ismaili community came to be formed in Balochistan and Sindh. Ismailis from Iran dropped anchor at Gwadar, Pasni, Ormara and Jiwani. Some went to Muscat because part of what is today Balochistan, including the port city of Gwadar, was under the ruler of Oman. The family of my maternal grandfather, Qasim, chose to settle down in Gwadar and my mother, Zaverbai, was born there years later. Still later, when I grew up and began my business, I made numerous visits to Gwadar and it became a milestone in my career. Each visit had an emotional imprint, as this was the first home of my dear mother. About 150 years ago, the town of Las Bela had emerged as the seat of a vibrant Ismaili community in Balochistan and in the area bordering Sindh. Las Bela is a remarkable city that has found mention in history books at various stages, centuries removed from each other. It is said that between the times of Alexander the Great— who passed Las Bela on his journey back from Punjab (Pakistan and India) to Babylon—and a British official in the nineteenth century, no European had seen Las Bela. In the eighth century, the Arab general Mohammed bin Qasim crossed Las Bela on his way to the Islamic conquest of Sindh.

Mukhi Tharoo came to live in either Las Bela or Sonmiani, a coastal town in south-east Balochistan, about 150 km from Karachi. The family is not certain but Mukhi Tharoo is probably buried in Sonmiani, now a centre for Pakistan's nascent space industry. We know very little about what Mukhi Tharoo did for a living or where exactly he lived. We have access only to sketchy oral records and stories passed down in the family. I have tried to engage local historians and Ismaili elders to find out more about Mukhi Tharoo and his family in Las Bela and in Sonmiani but, so far, my efforts have not been fruitful. What we can guess is that he was respected in the community. The honorific 'Mukhi' implies he led the faithful in prayer and presided over the *jamaatkhana*—the congregational location where Ismailis gather for worship. His son, Mukhi Hashoo, performed a similar religious role, since he too succeeded to his father's title. Mukhi Hashoo subsequently moved to Karachi, where he started a small business, trading in wool and animal skin.

One day, his destiny changed. A British gentleman, on a business trip to India, came to Mukhi Hashoo's office. He represented Ralli Brothers, a company that had earlier made small deals with Mukhi Hashoo and found him an honest man, true to his commitment. The visitor made Mukhi Hashoo an offer to become the sole supplier for Ralli Brothers, on a commission basis. He was to function like a house broker, procuring on behalf of his British principals. It was a critical breakthrough. Ralli Brothers was, at the time, one of the largest transcontinental mercantile houses and a driver of the global commodities trade. It was founded by five Greek brothers who had migrated to London and set up a new business there. They bought several items in Karachi—including wool and animal hides—in vast quantities and exported them to Europe. Now Mukhi Hashoo, my father's grandfather, was to be their sole representative. Obviously, he accepted the offer and worked hard and judiciously on their behalf. Eventually, he built a house in Karachi, in the Lea Market area, which I have now converted into the Hashoo Museum. Next door is a big jamaatkhana. This was important to Mukhi Hashoo, for he believed that the congregation and prayers to Allah were intrinsic to his identity and as much a part of his daily routine as his work. In fact, as his business grew, so did his charitable work and his promotion of the community. Many members of the *jamaat* from Las Bela were inspired to migrate to a better life in Karachi, a bigger city with a thriving seaport. When he died in 1911, Mukhi Hashoo had achieved a lot, combining temporal and religious obligations and being proud of his duties as a Mukhi till his last day.

For all his business acumen, Mukhi Hashoo was a simple, god-fearing, pious man. He had six sons (there may have been a seventh, we are not certain) and one daughter, Sharfi, the apple of his eye. She had a melodious voice and was acclaimed for her recitation and singing of *ginan*s and *kalaam*s, devotional poems and songs. Many proposals came for her but, for some reason, Mukhi Hashoo did not agree to any. Perhaps he thought, as so many doting fathers do, that his daughter deserved better than all the available suitors! One day, the legend goes, Mukhi Hashoo went to pay his respects to the Aga Khan. This was daily practice for him whenever the Aga Khan visited Karachi from Bombay. Mukhi Hashoo was very close to the Aga Khan—this was probably His Highness Aga Khan III, the 48th Imam—and called on him at his hilltop house, charmingly named Honeymoon Lodge. On his return journey, in his horse carriage, Mukhi Hashoo began weeping. A *jamaatbhai*—a paid servitor who looked after the jamaatkhana—found him in tears and asked him what was wrong. It appeared that the Aga Khan had rebuffed him and asked why his daughter was not married yet. The tone was polite but the disapproval was obvious. 'This is the first time the Aga Khan is upset with me,' Mukhi Hashoo said, 'I will agree to the first proposal I get.' As it happened, the jamaatbhai had a son, a widower of humble economic conditions; he asked for Sharfi's hand for his son. Mukhi Hashoo agreed at once. When he went home and announced his decision, his

10

sons, Sharfi's brothers, protested but their father would hear none of it. The following morning, he visited the Imam again and informed him: 'I fixed the marriage of my daughter yesterday.' The Aga Khan smiled and said, 'May Allah bless you . . . Sharfi's children will smell like roses.' Despite these words, there were doubters when Sharfi got married because not much was expected of her husband and their future. However, she did produce beautiful, wonderful, accomplished children. One of them was Ghulam Ali Allana (1906–85), writer and poet, scholar and diplomat, a close friend of the Quaid-e-Azam and a man with a long and distinguished career in the service of Pakistan and at the United Nations (UN). Towards the end of his life, in 1977, Allana was nominated for the Nobel Peace Prize for his work as chair of the UN Commission on Human Rights. He was an immensely popular and well-liked man, and it was once said of him that 'he smelt like a rose'. The Aga Khan's prophecy had come true! I suppose this is destiny, this is fate.

The belief that God determines our trajectory before He sends us to this world runs deep among members of my family. I was born to pious parents and this sense of submission to Allah is a part of my legacy. My parents were practising but practical religious people. This was what they had learnt from their parents. While they were believers and devout Muslims, my parents also

11

imbibed the tolerance and inclusiveness that the Prophet preached. When the Prophet conquered Mecca and took charge of the Kaaba shrine, he did not stop non-Muslims from practising their faiths. The Quran does not force anybody to adhere to Islam; conversion to the faith has to be a product of one's own conviction. That is why my parents felt their children should appreciate Islam not merely because they were born into a Muslim family but because they had come to understand and imbibe the essence of the faith of their own accord. I must confess that this has happened with me as well. I am a more serious Muslim now. I have struggled and worked hard, lived a challenging life, earned honestly, spoken truthfully and aspired for transparency. For inspiration to do this, and for greater contentment, I have found myself increasingly turning to religion. I suppose somewhere inside me lives on the legacy of Mukhi Hashoo, who so magically combined his piety and his professional chores. One thing that I know is *haraam* (forbidden) in Islam is jealousy. Unfortunately, I have seen too much of it in my personal life and in Pakistan, experienced it, suffered its consequences. Frankly, I can think of nothing more un-Islamic than jealousy and envy. I know I have digressed from the linear story of the family but the preceding passage was important to convey, as the colloquial expression goes, 'where I come from', and the spiritual as well as day-to-day lessons I learnt from my parents, especially my mother.

Following Mukhi Hashoo's death, his son Abdullah took charge of the business and continued to be a house broker for Ralli Brothers. On Abdullah's passing in 1927, his son—my father, Hussain—took over the family firm. In a few years, he was joined by my eldest brother, Akbar. By now, the mainstay of their trade was cotton, of which they were procuring impressive volumes. This business continued for another half-century, till Ralli Brothers shut down operations in Pakistan in 1968. Akbar worked with them till the very end. My father, who died in 1977, had of course retired by 1968. My father was my early role model. He was always busy and took the business to new heights. The 46th Imam, Aga Khan I, had settled down in Bombay, as I wrote, and died and was buried there. Since my father's family was close to him and his successors and often visited them to pay respects or for consultations, there was constant travel between Karachi and Bombay. My father, Hussain, was born on one such journey, when his parents were coming back by boat from Bombay. It was a family joke that my father's fondness for ships—he was absolutely riveted by them and the idea of sea travel and cargo-carrying vessels—stemmed from his being born on a ferry!

Hussain had a large family of seven children—four girls and three boys. I was number six, followed by my younger sister. In 1939, the year before I was born, my father built his house in Karachi. Known as 'Green Bungalow', it was the only one in Mithadar area and quite a landmark in the neighbourhood. While most others in the area lived in flats, my father managed to build a house, an indicator of the relative prosperity of the family following the association with Ralli Brothers. It was seen as an achievement and a subject of pride among the Ismaili community. Sir Sultan Muhammed Shah, His Highness Aga Khan III—the 48th Imam, grandfather of the current and 49th Imam—came to Karachi to inaugurate the bungalow. The following year, I was born in Jan Bai Maternity Home—today known as Aga Khan Hospital for Women and Children—about 2 km from Green Bungalow, near Kharadar Jamaatkhana. Our neighbourhood was a model civic community, with its unity, charity and spirit of volunteerism. It was a happy and simple world to be born into, as the 1940s beckoned. Little were my parents to know that the following decade would change their lives and the history of their community and country, forever.

1

BUILDING BLOCKS

Looking after a large family of seven children, in addition to supporting various cousins and distant relatives, was not easy on Hussain, my father. The Second World War, which broke out in Europe just before I was born, made its presence felt in Asia by 1942. My father's business was brought to its knees. The market for commodities in Europe contracted appreciably. That apart, transcontinental shipping was affected and prone to attacks by naval vessels from hostile countries. This was a bleak period for the Ralli Brothers brokerage in Karachi and for the city generally. Being a port city and a centre of commerce for centuries, Karachi was highly dependent on global trade currents. When the world economy suffered, so did Karachi. As far back as the close of the nineteenth century, it was already the biggest wheat-exporting port east of the Suez Canal. This prosperity and openness to trade winds gave it a cosmopolitan polish, an ease of manner and a verve and spirit that was unmatched in other Pakistani cities that were its contemporaries. Other than Muslims, the city had substantial communities of Christians, Parsis, Jews and, of course, Hindus—though many left for India in 1947, when two new nations were created out of the British Empire. During the Second World War, 30,000 Polish refugees, escaping their country after the horrific invasion by Hitler's Nazis, fled to Karachi where they were welcomed by the locals. This added to the vibrancy and pluralism of the city when I was still a little boy. I often relate this story to friends as an example of the hospitality and welcoming nature of Pakistanis. It is not just the Afghan refugees who have been with us since the Soviet occupation of Kabul in 1979; years before that, we opened our doors to troubled and forsaken people from as far away as Eastern Europe. As a thanksgiving to Karachi, a group of Polish air veterans came to Pakistan shortly after its birth and helped set up Pakistan Air Force.

The Second World War ended in 1945 but history continued to take other momentous turns. I was a small boy then and my family was ordinary, middle class; we were far removed from the great movements of power and politics. Even so, we realized that something dramatic was soon to come. The British Raj was ending and the viceroy and his officers were going home. They would leave behind a free Pakistan, a new nation: our nation. The story of why British India was partitioned is well documented and has been the subject of many scholarly works and books. I don't want to delve into that because it is not really relevant here. Yet, I must emphasize that the Ismaili community was invested in the idea of Pakistan and the quest for a separate homeland for the Muslims of British India, one where they could live with dignity and develop their society without the influence of the Hindu-dominated politics of the Congress party, which came to rule independent India. The movement for the creation of Pakistan was spearheaded by the Muslim League, of which Quaid-e-Azam Mohammad Ali Jinnah was the most charismatic leader in the mid-1940s. The Muslim League had been founded in 1906 by His Highness, Aga Khan III, Sir Sultan Muhammed Shah, the 48th Imam. He served as its first president and was a proponent of education, social upliftment and political rights—leading to a separate nation—for the Muslims of British India. As such, when Pakistan was created on 14 August 1947, it was a matter of special pride for Ismailis because the Aga Khan had worked so hard towards that. In those early days, when money was scarce, Aga Khan III stood like a rock behind the Quaid-e-Azam, giving him political and diplomatic support and helping financially to pay for administrative expenses and government salaries. A decade later, in 1958, Prince Aly Khan served as Pakistan's ambassador to the UN. Aly Khan was the son of the 48th Imam and the father of the current and 49th Imam, His Highness, Prince Karim Aga Khan.

I was too young to comprehend the birth of my nation, being a boy of only seven. I did overhear the family elders as they talked, but understood little. This was an era before 24×7 TV, Justice Iftikhar Chaudhary and the news media boom. People still got their news from local newspapers and, more than that, by talking to each other. What I do remember and what still sends a tingling sensation down my spine is the sense of optimism and euphoria. Pakistan was not too industrialized; it was a predominantly agricultural country. It was a new nation, with limited capital and infrastructural gaps, especially in rural and interior regions. Even so, there was buoyancy and hope—for freedom and self-respect, for jobs and education, for individual growth and social development. The Quaid-e-Azam was a much loved man who had a modern outlook. He was also a seasoned politician. This was just the combination a young Pakistan needed, and his people—the citizens of the country he had helped form—adored him. As a Muslim nation emerging from colonization, Pakistan attracted goodwill and empathy from Muslim peoples everywhere, from Turkey to the Arab countries, from West Asia to east Africa. This was because it was perceived as an embodiment of the hopes and aspirations of not just its citizens but of the Islamic community everywhere.

Help and know-how was willingly shared, and Muslims from far away were drawn to Pakistan. Let me illustrate with an example. The Fancy family was among the first major business houses in Pakistan. They came to Karachi in 1947, just before our independence, and settled there, having sold off their business interests in Kenya and other parts of Africa. True, commercial imperatives may have appealed to the Fancy family—they were fellow Ismailis—but clearly there was also an emotional commitment to Pakistan that brought them to Karachi. I am not relating this story to flatter or praise my friends. In fact, in subsequent years, I was to compete with the companies of the Fancy Group. The point I am trying to make is that Pakistan started off with limited physical resources but with limitless affection from its friends. It had a lot going for it back then, in 1947, and if it couldn't capitalize on that, it has to—and we Pakistanis have to—look within, and we cannot merely wring our hands and blame external factors.

The partition of British India and the birth of Pakistan resulted in a two-way migration: Muslims came to Pakistan from India and Hindus left Pakistan for India. In the period leading up to August 1947, there was brutal violence. It was at its bloodiest in Punjab and Bengal—two British Indian provinces that were divided between Pakistan and India—but even Karachi saw its share. This was unfortunate and has left wounds between our two countries that have regrettably still not healed. Karachi's demographic profile began to change as many of our Muslim brothers and sisters arrived as refugees and migrants predominantly from the plains of northern India. There were smaller groups of arrivals from southern, eastern and western India. They came with prayers on their lips and hopes in their hearts, for this new nation that we would share and build.

These tumultuous transformations had a minor impact on my family. After the Second World War, as the economy and trade began to recover, my father redoubled his efforts at work. Ralli Brothers remained his focus. When the business had gone into cotton procurement and trade, my father had felt the need to take on a partner. This was Moolchand Lilaram, a Hindu. In 1947, Moolchand Lilaram took his family to India, leaving behind a piece of land near what is now Mazar-e-Quaid or the Jinnah Mausoleum, the final resting place of Pakistan's founding father. As can be imagined, this was and still is prime property. When Moolchand Lilaram departed, he left my father in charge of the land. 'I give you the land in trust,' he said. 'If I come back, return it to me. Otherwise it is yours.' My father took him by the hand and promised, 'I will look after your land but never transfer it to my name.' Moolchand Lilaram and his family never came back—but my father was true to his word and did not take ownership of or lay claim to the property. Today, that piece of land belongs to the Pakistan government. Another Hindu businessman, Khushi Ram, was a partner of my father's. He stayed on in Karachi, one among a handful of Hindu families that remained. Khushi Ram continued to be a part of the business till the Ralli Brothers shut down operations in Pakistan in 1968. I had no personal experience of the cross-migration, of the departure of Hindus and the arrival of Muslims from other parts of British India. I was, as I said, much too young. What I do remember with some poignancy is that the shops that sold me toys emptied out. All of them happened to be owned and run by Hindu shopkeepers.

Being the second-youngest in a household of seven children had its advantages. I was much loved by my parents and had older siblings who doted on me. The age gap was fairly sharp. My parents' firstborn, my sister, was eleven years my senior. The older of my two brothers, Akbar, was born eight years before me. By 1947, while I was still a small boy running around and playing on the streets, Akbar was already being introduced to the business and accompanying my father to work. It was clear that, as the eldest son, he would inherit the Ralli Brothers brokerage. Akbar now lives in Karachi with his three sons and a daughter. We have gone our own ways, and life has taken us in different directions.

I was closer to my second brother, Hasan Ali, who died tragically young in 1974 in London. He too had three sons and a daughter. On his deathbed, he asked Akbar to look after them. However, I took on the responsibility and brought up his children as my own. Later his former wife—Hasan Ali had got divorced a few years before he died—took me to court in an action that stunned and hurt me but that's another story. Incidentally, large families seem to be a Hashwani trait. I myself have five children: three girls and two boys.

In the early 1950s, Akbar got married to Ghulam Ali Allana's daughter. Green Bungalow was too small for the expanded family and we moved into a bigger house in Karachi's Soldier Bazaar area. This was a four-bedroom house, which my father rented for 125 rupees a month, a large sum in those days. While the older girls were married off and Akbar helped my father at work, the younger siblings were busy with school, for my parents were determined to equip us with a good education. We weren't very rich and business was tough in a Pakistan that was building itself as an independent economy. There was no retinue of servants waiting on us; we had to chip in with chores. As a seven- or eight-year-old, I can remember going to the evening shift of NJV High School—or

Narayan Jagannath Vaidya High School, to give its full name—the oldest government school in Sindh. My siblings used to go to morning school but, for some reason, I was enrolled in the evening shift. This meant that I was sent out to buy groceries in the morning, after which I was to help my mother clean the house. After that, I would walk a few kilometres to Bolton Market, in Mithadar area, get on a tram and reach school by 1 p.m. On coming back home, I would help my mother iron the clothes—which she had washed while I was in school—and then polish my shoes. It was a fixed routine, and the grounding in housework and cleanliness was to stand me in good stead. Several times in my hotels, when I see a speck of dust or some crumpled paper on the floor, I reach out and set things right on my own, without calling out for someone. I still clean my own shoes and iron my clothes in a hotel room, pulling out the ironing board and getting to work. My mother would have been proud. I didn't know it then but she was imparting early lessons in self-sufficiency.

I had lasting individual relationships with both my parents. Though my father was busy through the week, he still made an effort to find time for me. On Saturday evenings, he would take me out to dinner and show me the wonders of glittering Karachi, the City of Lights. We would walk to the port side, where he would point out the ships to me and then to the bustling shopping area in Sadar. There we would have a light dinner and come home after a nice and happy outing. Those were the simple pleasures of life. On bigger occasions, when there was cause for a special celebration, the family used to go to the popular Clifton Beach and then for dinner to Bolton Market, invariably to the famous Sindh Islamia restaurant.

It was my parents who taught me the importance of contributing to social causes. There was milk shortage in Pakistan in those days and the US government used to send milk powder, the packets marked with an emblem. I was given the task of making milk with the powder and distributing it to poor people in the area. Right after, we would go for prayers, which my father, as the Mukhi, used to lead. From my father I learnt humility. He was calm and polite to a fault, always smiling and never complaining, not even in the midst of the most difficult crisis. The one word you kept hearing from him was *shukr* ('thanks')—directed at his fellow human beings and at the Almighty. Truly, the greatest blessing is for someone to have shukr in his heart for it suggests contentment and represents the mercy of Allah. It is the external articulation of an inner peace. Those who live in such a frame of mind are blessed, and my father was.

My mother was the backbone of the family. She was also the treasurer, learning to keep the house going on a strict budget. This meant she had to be extremely disciplined and make every paisa count. There was no wastefulness or indulgence for her when it came to financial matters. She trimmed unnecessary expenses; there was only one servant to help with household chores. She cooked as well as washed our clothes. Thrift was a habit that lingered from the austere days of the Second World War. To supplement my father's income, my mother began to buy cloth from the wholesale Bolton Market and sell it in the neighbourhood. She even stitched clothes for family and friends, with me running the machine for her. We had many conversations about life while together. She used to tell me, *'Band mutthi lakh ki, khul gayi to khaak ki.'* (The closed palm is worth a lakh rupees, but the open palm is worth nothing.) I spoke to my mother in Sindhi, the language we used at home. When alone, I spoke to her in Balochi—which my mother knew because of her Gwadar background and which she taught me. Other languages I picked up as a child were Gujarati and Punjabi and, of course, Urdu and English.

I was a sickly child and perhaps that was why I was sent to evening school—so that my mother could watch over me while the other children were away in the morning. I suffered a gamut of diseases—smallpox, mumps, frequent high fevers and appendicitis, which led to an appendectomy at the age of fourteen. The most painful of all was the tonsillitis operation at fifteen, in the clinic of Dr Habib Patel, a well-known Karachi surgeon and a

distant relative of the Indian businessman Azim Premji.
Dr Patel had taken out my appendix the previous year. He
was an accomplished medical practitioner but must have
found me an extremely stubborn patient. I refused to use
chloroform before my appendicitis surgery. 'Why should
I be put to sleep?' I asked, 'I would rather watch.' The
alternative course was a big injection in my spinal cord
to numb the body. I stayed awake during the operation,
much to my parents' amazement. Call it determination
or foolish rigidity—whatever it was, that was how I was.
A year later, I went back to Dr Patel because my tonsils
had to be removed. I was again offered chloroform
and again I said 'No'. The alternative was a number of
injections in my inner throat, the syringe shoved into
my open mouth. It sounds terrible and it was. It became
quite a theatre that day in the hospital. The doctor and
hospital staff members were caught unawares by this
refusal to use chloroform and one of them said I was a
'mad boy'. It was for the first time that the hospital had
used the multiple injection mechanism as no patient
had rejected chloroform before. Anyway, it worked and
Dr Patel removed my enlarged tonsils. Cotton bandages
were inserted to heal the wound. They were to be taken
out about a week later, when the skin had recovered and
been stitched together. The process of pulling out the
cotton bandages—necessitated by my insistence on the

use of injections—was very painful. It left me with tears in my eyes. Even so, it convinced the family that I had an obstinate streak in me and that once I had made up my mind, nothing could change it.

My mother hoped this determination would translate into scholastic excellence but I let her down. While I enjoyed some subjects, I simply didn't take the classroom seriously. I went through a series of schools, including a primary school near the house and then Aga Khan School in Kharadar, before moving to NJV High School from where I took my matriculation examination. My closest friend at NJV was Hari Jejasia, who topped our class and became a chartered accountant in Toronto. I met him in Dubai in 2013 and discovered that his son—Hari married an Englishwoman—worked for the government of Abu Dhabi and was, in a sense, my neighbour in Dubai. Hari and I shared a lot, including a passion for mathematics, my favourite subject. However, much of my time was spent on the sports field. On the streets outside my house, I learnt the indigenous sport of *gilli-danda* and tennis-ball cricket. My interest in cricket grew into an obsession and I worked hard at becoming a fast bowler, complete with a carefully cultivated temper. More a doer than a theorist, I kept myself busy, not by reading or immersing myself in encyclopedias but simply by doing things with my hands. I kept a pet dog and gave it a bath every day. I kept a pet hen and checked if it had laid eggs, every day. I planted roses in our little patch and began a lifelong love for gardening. Every house I have built or lived in has been blessed with a garden—I have ensured that. Alas Allah does not permit me the time to water the plants myself! As a boy, I also enjoyed pottering around the kitchen. If chicken was being cooked, I would slaughter the bird myself and clean up the mess. Cleanliness, as I said earlier, is a fetish with me, inherited from my mother.

My mother was a clever woman. She realized that Akbar would take charge of the Ralli Brothers business and there would be no place for me in my father's company. I would have to chart out an independent career path. She was keen that I become a doctor. In 1956, after graduating from NJV High School, I was admitted to the Sindh Muslim (SM) Science College for the pre-medical course. Among my subjects were biology, chemistry and literature. I was good at chemistry and biology while literature was my weakness. I had a lackadaisical attitude, though, and didn't pay these subjects the attention they deserved. The freedom of college life had an electrifying effect on me and I developed a busy extracurricular schedule. I bought a Chinese-made bicycle for 142 rupees and spent the day cycling around the city, from college to cricket matches to gallivanting trips. Students' union activities kept me from my books, much to my mother's annoyance.

I lived and breathed cricket: playing seven days a week, listening to radio commentary, collecting pictures of cricketers. As a fast bowler, my reputation grew in local tournaments, played on matting wickets in the 1950s. Apart from my college, I played for the Aga Khan Gymkhana. Our team won the Karachi Cricket Association Gold Cup in 1958, beating a strong Pakistan International Airlines (PIA) team in the final. We scored 149 runs in 50 overs and bowled out PIA, which had nine cricketers who had represented Pakistan XI, for a paltry 65. My fast bowling played a crucial role in our victory. We were a boisterous lot, once barging into a ladies' tea party at the Gymkhana, right after a cricket match, and finishing off the sandwiches and other food before the ladies realized what was happening! I have often been asked if I ever seriously considered a career in cricket. Frankly, the thought never occurred to me. There was no money in cricket in those days, no endorsements, no sponsorships, no razzmatazz. It was not the glamour magnet it is today. Tellingly, not one cricketer from the talented Aga Khan Gymkhana team of my generation made it to the top of the sport or to Test and international cricket. The reason was simple enough: cricket was not professionally rewarding. To pursue a career in cricket, one needed to be backed by family money or a government or army job. Middle-class Ismaili boys typically came from families that ran small businesses or wanted to push their children into education and white-collar jobs. Cricket was a luxury they couldn't afford in the long run. Even when some of my teammates leveraged cricket skills to join institutions like Habib Bank or National Bank of Pakistan or PIA, soon enough they began to focus on the core office job and stay away from the 22-yard pitch. Salaries, promotion prospects, higher incomes, a family to support: these were the priorities that were ingrained in us by our parents. It is remarkable that despite the popularity of cricket among Ismailis, the first member of the community to play for Pakistan was Salim Jaffer, who made his Test debut as recently as 1986. Coincidentally, he was also a fast bowler. When I saw him bowl, I did feel a small twinge of regret. The whites on the ground, the shiny red ball, the pace bowler marking his run-up, the crowd roaring: could this have been my destiny? The thought lasted only a moment. It was Allah's wish that I give up cricket; He had another innings in mind for me.

The carefree days were drawing to a close and, in 1958, my final examination loomed at SM Science College. How well I did would determine whether I got into medical college and went on to become a doctor, as my mother so wanted. I remember it was the day after my chemistry practical. I liked the chemistry laboratory and used to spend hours there. The test had gone well and I was satisfied. The following morning was the examination in literature—not my forte. Suddenly I had a panic attack. On examination day, I was blank. I telephoned a friend early in the morning and sought his help. He lived far away and was a model student—born into a poor family, he worked part-time as a telephone operator to pay his college fees and yet found time for his books. He cycled a considerable distance to come and see me. I placed the prescribed text—R.L. Stevenson's *Dr Jekyll and Mr Hyde*—in his hands and asked, 'What is this? What is inside it?' I had not read it. He looked puzzled. 'It will take days to read it and explain it to you,' he responded. 'You know we don't have the time,' I said, 'so just give me the gist, some points . . . Please!' When the results came, I had scored 11 on 100. I needed 33 marks to pass. Since I'd failed, there was no question of admission to a medical college. My mother was distraught and very, very angry. For the first time in my life, she slapped me. Her dream had been shattered—her little boy was not going to be a doctor.

Immensely practical, my mother began to think quickly. She realized I wasn't going to study and that planning an academic future for me was fruitless. She knew there was no vacancy in my father's business, as my brother Akbar was already too well ensconced in it. Betting on her instincts, she pulled me out of college and requested my brother-in-law Shamshuddin, who ran a small food trading business, to take me on as an apprentice. Shamshuddin was married to my eldest sister, Malik Sultan, and was some twenty years my senior. Working with him would, my mother hoped, straighten me out and, as they say, make a man of her boy. There was no arguing with my mother when she had taken a decision. My father agreed to her plan. He was the quiet one and submitted to her when it came to critical family matters. So off I was sent, one day in 1958, to Shamshuddin's.

My boyhood was over.

2

MY OWN APPRENTICE

Shamshuddin was much older than me and with him being the husband of the first of my sisters, the relationship had a certain formality to it. In our part of the world, particularly in Pakistan, sons-in-law and brothers-in-law are given almost deferential treatment and spoken to with utmost regard. On the other hand, Shamshuddin was not quite a stranger. He was part of a joint family that my parents had known for years. He lived and worked with his brothers and cousins and their families, in the Lasi Jamaatkhana area, an indicator that they too had migrated from Las Bela like many other Ismaili families of Karachi. Shamshuddin and his family had several businesses but the bulk of their earnings came from exporting dried fish to Colombo, the capital of Sri Lanka. The Makran Coast, which overlaps Sindh and Balochistan provinces in Pakistan, is rich in fish and this made Karachi a centre for fish and seafood commerce. Shamshuddin's father had been involved in the fish trade for years and had, in fact, migrated from Ormara, then a small fishing hamlet in Las Bela, to Bela (the largest town in Las Bela district) before finally settling down in Karachi. Following his marriage to my sister, Shamshuddin sought to carve out a niche for himself, free of the family businesses that his father had already established. At this stage, my parents helped him and put up enough capital to make my brother Hasan Ali, six years my senior, and Shamshuddin equal partners in a joint venture (JV).

The JV didn't last very long because my brother's personal life took an interesting turn when he got married to a doctor from Colombo. My new sister-in-law, an Ismaili girl with origins in Kutch (today Gujarat in India), lived with her family in Sri Lanka, where they had migrated to years earlier. My entire family sailed from Karachi to Colombo for the wedding but I stayed behind. My father's brothers—Husain Ali and Noor Mohammad, both unmarried—were staying with me at our Soldier Bazaar house. Husain Ali was not well and I was tending to him. Unfortunately, he died even as the wedding celebrations were under way in Colombo. Rather than disturb my parents and interrupt the wedding, I took charge and ensured the burial and other rites proceeded as they should. So I met my sister-in-law Laila only after she came home with the bridegroom's party.

Laila knew Karachi quite well. She had studied to be a doctor in the city, after her schooling in Colombo. Even so, to her, Karachi was a temporary home; she wanted to go to London for further studies. My brother, soft-spoken and dominated by his wife, agreed to accompany her and give her the support she needed as a medical student and a wife. They would be gone for at least two years. It was a big sacrifice and unusual for a man in the 1950s. In a sense, my brother was enlightened and far ahead of his time. However, his departure meant he would not be able to honour the obligations of his agreement with Shamshuddin. That was when I was asked to fill the gap and take over Hasan Ali's partnership with Shamshuddin, in Southern Commercial Corporation (SCC).

The business involved handling the transport and distribution of food grains on behalf of the ministry of food, Government of Sindh, to far-flung coastal towns of Balochistan. These were relatively poor towns, in arid, desert locations, where local agricultural produce was scarce. The people were dependent on food brought in from other parts of Pakistan. While the business was structured as a fifty–fifty partnership, Shamshuddin took ample advantage of his experience and of the age gap.

Bluntly speaking, he didn't treat me fairly and made me do the donkey's share of the work—running around, sorting out logistical details, travelling constantly, spending hours in office, ensuring dispatches. He ordered me around and did precious little himself. The foodgrains were being dispatched to Balochistan, the business was based in Sindh, and the clients in a sense involved governments and authorities in both provinces. This made for an intricate matrix. I had to go to Kalat to collect and process the bills. Then I would proceed to Mastung, near Quetta (capital of Balochistan), where the nearest branch of the National Bank of Pakistan was located, to get the pay order. There were no courier services or emails in those days; even telephones were a luxury. In the interiors of Balochistan, the post office network was not rigorous. All this had to be done in person.

Every two weeks, I would leave Karachi for my hopping tour of Balochistan. I would pay twenty-five rupees for an ordinary berth—it used to be called 'inter-class'—on Bolan Mail that left Karachi station in the afternoon. I would be carrying some papers and clothes and my bedroll and would begin the slow trek into the heart of Balochistan. The name of the train itself—Bolan Mail—was evocative. The Bolan Pass is a spectacular work of nature and separates western Pakistan from Afghanistan. Nevertheless, there was nothing exciting about my journey on Bolan Mail or the errands I had to run. As the train trudged along, I would wait patiently for Kotri railway station, where we arrived in time for dinner. The train halted there for some time to replenish water and coal supplies for the steam engine. I would use the opportunity to have a quick dinner of *malai* (cream) and naan, for that was all that was available in this remote railway station so late in the evening. As the train resumed its journey, it would keep stopping at small stations. I would manage to sleep, occasionally waking up to try and get a cup of tea if the train had stopped, or just sit and stare out of the window into the darkness and fastness outside. In the middle of the night, almost always when I was sleeping, Bolan Mail would cross from Sindh into Balochistan. Early in the morning, the train would reach Sibi, a Baloch town with a long and illustrious history. Here I would have breakfast—a boiled egg and a slice of bread, with a welcome and hot cup of tea. Then the train would move again, with me invariably having to run to catch it, having gulped down the last of my cup of tea and hurriedly paid for breakfast. At noon, I would reach Quetta, after an 850-km trip.

The reason for my train journey was prosaic and confined to collecting bills and seeking payments. The railway tracks that Bolan Mail and I used, though, were of enormous strategic significance. They had been laid by the British in the 1870s and 1880s to allow rapid movement of troops and military logistics and to guard against Russian adventurism—or a possible invasion—in Afghanistan. These thoughts and those geopolitical games were far from my mind as I began travelling to Balochistan, but little was I to know that nineteenth-century strategic calculations were to reappear and haunt Pakistan only a quarter-century later!

Just outside Quetta railway station, I would have a relatively relaxed lunch of *saalan* (meat curry) and roti. Once my work in the city was done, I would clamber on to the bus to Kalat. The bus was actually a four-wheel truck converted into some sort of a mass transit vehicle. I would try to get a seat in front, dressed in my overcoat, for the weather was cold and temperatures dropped below freezing point in winter. Summer would be pleasant in comparison, even if some days got very hot, with temperatures climbing to 40°C. The drive to Kalat would take six hours and we would reach well into the evening. No time to waste . . . As soon as I put my bags in a very basic room rented at the government guest house, it would be time to sort out the paperwork, follow up on the billing and processing, and meet and renew acquaintances with the civil servants responsible for clearing my documents and releasing our payment the following day. Dinner too would usually be saalan and roti and, especially in winter, would herald a cold and uncomfortable night. The bedroom, a large hall converted into a sleeping area for five rupees a night, would be lit with candles. For heating, I would have to make do with four pieces of wood burning in that large room. It would never be enough to keep me warm and the embers would seldom survive the night. Electricity was still a rarity and, in Kalat, limited to three hours of supply every evening. This was my initiation into the world of work and business travel. It was tough, it was educative and, in its own way, it was fun.

It was also crucial to our little business. Margins were small. Following bill collection and release of pay orders, we would have just enough rollover capital for the next transaction. Once the money came in, it was my task to take delivery of the next round of foodgrains in Karachi, ensure it was loaded on to country crafts, and send it off to coastal towns such as Pasni, Ormara and Gwadar. Labourers would carry the sacks on their backs. I had to be there in person to ensure there was no delay or pilferage. Sometimes, I would carry sacks of grain myself to encourage the others and push things along. In Gwadar and Pasni, there were no landing berths and the grain had to be loaded on to smaller boats by labourers—else, we would carry the sacks through the waters to land. All of us—I was present for the unloading occasionally—would get our trousers and legs wet in the shallow waters. It wasn't always a pleasant sight but somewhere, somehow, this treadmill experience was making a man of me. A few days after the foodgrains had been sent, I would go to Pasni, Gwadar and the other points of delivery to get a receipt or a certificate that the stock had arrived in good order. After that, I would return to Karachi and prepare the invoices, before boarding Bolan Mail and beginning the rocky return journey to Quetta, Kalat, and payday.

Shamshuddin was putting me through the wringer. Though his intentions may not always have been straightforward, in retrospect, I am grateful for all that the Balochistan trips taught me. One night, I was on the back of a truck, travelling from Gwadar to Turbat. It was past midnight on a sandy, unsteady road and silence enveloped us. Suddenly the truck shuddered to a stop. It had broken down. It was dark and desolate outside. Bereft of tools and spare parts, the driver gave up. We would have to camp there for the night, he announced. Some of the passengers protested, and arguments began. I was too tired to say anything. Opening up my bedroll and stowing my steel trunk—with my precious documents—under my feet, I went off to sleep on the sands of Balochistan, with the sky as my top sheet. When I woke up, my face had been bitten most meticulously by desert insects. I had been too exhausted to notice and had snored on while the insects had got down to their business!

Those journeys on Bolan Mail and on souped-up trucks were my introduction to Balochistan, a part of my country where my forefathers had stayed for some years but a part I just didn't know. I went through a gamut of emotions—exhilaration, sentimentalism, even anger on seeing the poverty in Balochistan. Coming from a big city, with a full and active life, it was my first time in the countryside. I saw the barren lands and the tiny villages of Balochistan from the window of a moving train, from the seat of a truck-cum-bus, while walking down the lanes of Kalat and Pasni, and many other towns, each steeped in history and telling a thousand stories. There were sparse, open stretches of sand that seemed to go on for ever yet gripped me with their stark splendour. Gwadar was special because it was where my mother hailed from. What struck me was the poverty there. It was an eye-opener. The sight of children walking barefoot on the hot sands; the starvation and the protruding bellies; the fact that donkey carts were the most common mode of transport and you could travel for hours without seeing a car; the denial of water, of education: it shook me. It was clear our government was failing its people and letting down the poor of Balochistan. Deep inside, my idealism about one composite Pakistani society, where the state and the 'system' treated all equally, began to be questioned. I felt grateful to Allah because I was better off, but I was also very angry. What made things more poignant was the innocence of the people. Despite their rough-and-ready ways and their nomadic existence, the Baloch people were simple-minded and warm to strangers. It was notable that there was comparatively little crime and the roads were safe even at night. On my part, I conversed with ordinary people and those I met on the streets in Balochi, honing my skills in the language and thanking my mother every day for tutoring me in it. Regrettably, Balochistan hasn't changed in these past fifty years. It remains a province of much potential but also much poverty, marked by poor delivery of public services.

Meanwhile, my efforts were paying off and SCC was being nursed to robust health. The business started making money and its reputation grew. I was working round the clock, much to the amazement of my mother and college friends who had known me from my days of cricket and extracurricular activities. In the office, I was accountant, dispatcher, manager, peon, general dogsbody, everything. My brother-in-law would come in at 10 a.m. and lounge around till 1 p.m., occasionally asking unnecessary questions. Then he would go to his club for a leisurely lunch, come back around 3 p.m., mooch about for an hour and then go home. My hours were much longer, and our margins too began to fatten with my hours at work. Let me put it thus: SCC began to blossom. I soon felt it was time to diversify. Shamshuddin had no opinion on the matter and I pushed ahead, knowing I would be doing the work in any case. I signed a contract for delivering stevedoring services and clearing ships on behalf of the federal government's ministry of food and agriculture, which imported wheat through Karachi port. We won the contract on a competitive basis, having bid the lowest for a business we had no experience in. Now I had to teach myself to become a customs agent and clearance facilitator, and interact with the federal government—a long leap from officials of the provincial government. It was a make-or-break moment.

We handled our first ship in 1959. I still remember the name, *Hellenic Glory*, for it had me thinking of ancient Greece and of the task of Hercules. *Hellenic Glory* brought in 8000 tonnes of wheat. Once the wheat had been delivered, I had to make myself familiar with the government officials who would pay my fee. Certificate of delivery, bill processing, payment collection: the cycle started again, only this time it required me to visit federal government officials. The stevedore business flourished and we found we needed more space. So we moved out of our Kagzi Bazaar premises to a spanking new office in Habib Square. More staff was recruited in anticipation of growth. In all this, we deployed the profits from the Balochistan operations and did not borrow fresh capital. My hard work was beginning to pay dividends. My transformation to a serious worker from a happy-go-lucky teen, who could even have been described as a shirker, amazed many who had known me earlier. With the zeal of a new convert, I became intolerant of failure and of taking it easy at work. Meeting targets and doing better and better were all that mattered. Something motivated me from within. Whatever it was, it kept me fully occupied: every week was a marathon.

Almost every day of the week saw us handle the unloading of wheat from a ship. Almost every day of the week saw us busy with Balochistan and its food transport and distribution business. Almost every day of the week saw me spend long hours outside office, either liaising with a government department or rolling up my sleeves at the port to supervise the loading or unloading of cargo, or travelling to Balochistan. It was hectic but I could feel a sense of happiness, of achievement. Colleagues and contemporaries began calling SCC a 'one-man show'. I laughed it off and continued with my work; business was booming and all was well with the world. Shamshuddin seemed a relaxed man. He was getting 50 per cent of the profit for very little work, and we were making enough to underwrite his club bills and his social life. It was a perfect arrangement for him—but in his mind, envy was plotting its own course.

One morning in 1961, as I was getting ready to go out and face another busy day, my mother called me and said she wanted to chat. I didn't take it seriously and was impatient to leave but something in her voice told me she had a serious matter to convey. Quietly, she explained that Malik Sultan had visited her and complained that I had stolen 5000 rupees from the safe at the SCC office. I had the key, since one of my many duties was that of cashier. Shamshuddin had told my sister (his wife) that 5000 rupees had gone missing overnight. The implication was that I was embezzling money and being dishonest. Obviously, this was a blatant lie. I was shell-shocked but my mother, pragmatic and sober in the stormiest circumstances, didn't wait for an explanation. She had gauged the situation and was already thinking ahead. 'If you stay,' she told me, 'your sister will have a problem.' I understood. That was my last day at the Habib Square office—I never went back. I never got my share of the profit or even the initial capital. All my profit had been reinvested in the company in the preceding months. Shamshuddin simply assumed 100 per cent ownership and control of the business, knowing that his parents-in-law and his brother-in-law would be too dignified to ask why. He ran the company but, without my determination and energy, there was no way SCC could have thrived, or even survived. Within a few years, Shamshuddin rendered it bankrupt.

By then, I was frying other fish.

3

THE SWINGING SIXTIES

Having been short-changed by Shamshuddin and left with
no money for a new business, I needed to start all over
again. The first opening I got was as a sales agent for the
Steel Corporation of Pakistan, owned by the Fancy family,
one of Pakistan's richest. My job was to sell bailing hoops
for cotton bales. To be honest, this wasn't really a job. I
was a sales agent and had to go to ginny factories to sell the
bailing hoops. The difference between the wholesale price
I paid Steel Corporation and the retail price my customer
paid me was my profit. Ginny factories produced cotton
using the spinning jenny, of which the word 'ginny' was a
derivative. They were familiar ground for me. By virtue of
my father's work with Ralli Brothers, the ginny factories

knew who I was. My father was a prominent buyer of their cotton. Though I had my father's goodwill, I did not have any capital.

To penetrate the ginny factories and do better than other agents, I had to be innovative. How did I do this? First, rather than pay Steel Corporation in cash, I began buying bailing hoops against cheques. Then I sent the bailing hoops to the warehouse or factory of the cotton manufacturer. I ensured that I got the delivery order at once from the factory manager; this confirmed that the bailing hoops had been received by my buyer. Next, I went personally to the ginny factory's owner, showed him the delivery order and collected my payment. I deposited this cheque into my account. I opened several bank accounts so that I could choose the bank account that was in the same bank or branch as that of my buyer. This ensured same-day credit—since the money had to be transferred from one account in the branch to another, it was done in a day's time. By the time Steel Corporation deposited the cheque I had issued to its managers, there was enough money in my account for my cheque to be honoured.

Why did I collect the cheques myself? Being a big company, Steel Corporation would have dispatched the cheque to its accounts department and waited a day before sending a peon or a clerk to the bank to deposit it. Also, it would not have got same-day credit, as my account and Steel Corporation's account were in different banks. When I rushed to deposit cheques personally and immediately, it gave me a time advantage and made up for my limited capital. I was lucky, I guess. In today's age of electronic transfers of money, there is little to distinguish a cheque issued from an account in the same branch, same bank, same city, or even same country. In the 1960s, things were different.

The two paragraphs you just read describe my strategy but don't entirely capture the gamut of my labours. As a sales agent, to be better than my competitors, I had to provide better service, not just push for quicker payments. This meant travelling to Steel Corporation's factory and taking physical delivery of the bailing hoops. I inspected each piece and picked up the best, rejecting any stock that was even slightly rusted. Steel Corporation's factory was 25 or 30 km from Karachi—a long distance in those days, when Pakistan's road infrastructure wasn't as developed. The loading at the factory was done in my presence. I negotiated with truck drivers and owners and bargained them down to reasonable rates. Every penny had to be counted and you had to keep an eye on cash flows. At the ginny factory, I made sure the manager assessed the bailing hoops and was satisfied with what he had received. Nobody taught me all this and I didn't know the jargon, but what I was doing was offering end-to-end solutions to my buyers and timely delivery. I also learnt to 'salute the customer twice', as I told a friend. The first time you saluted the owner of the ginny factory, because he gave you the order. The second time you saluted the chief accountant of the ginny factory, because he was responsible for issuing your cheque expeditiously. Times have changed, businesses have changed, my geographical frontiers have changed—but, believe me, some of those essential verities have not changed. Show me the businessman, anywhere in the world, who says he doesn't bother chasing up on payments and I will expose him for a liar!

My business as a sales agent for Steel Corporation of Pakistan grew over the following three or four years. From bailing hoops, I began selling other steel products—girders, steel bars, steel equipment for sugar factories—and built an expertise in the steel trade. Since steel began to engross me, I started to look at steel from not just the prism of Steel Corporation but beyond that. There was the option of buying and selling tinplate sheets and similar items. Pakistan used steel but was not necessarily self-sufficient in steel production. It had to import steel billets from North Korea, Japan and China. If you did your research and followed the commodity price swings, you could buy cheap and sell expensive. There was money in this trade but it was essential to educate oneself and capitalize on information arbitrage. I began to do that and, before long, found myself immersed in the steel trading business, without any background in it whatsoever.

Soon I was supplying steel billets—the feedstock—to steel products manufacturers and also buying their products, such as bailing hoops and girders, and selling them to end users. This gave me a fair grasp of the steel business and led to a logical extension when ginny factories made me an offer. I had been dealing with them for years and they had learnt to trust me. Two or three ginny factories approached me to sell their cotton in Karachi on a commission basis. They had seen my command over the commodities market—at least the steel end of it—and the effort I made to study price swings and so on. They felt I was well suited to manage a commodities trading operation by deploying my lessons from the steel trade in the cotton trade. Inspired somewhat by my father's own career in cotton procurement—and certain I could turn to him for advice when I ran into trouble—I agreed to the proposal. I started receiving consignments of cotton by train and truck from the ginny factories and had to find buyers for these. Here again, every lot had to be examined for quality. I had to be present at the time of unloading to ensure there was minimum leakage or damage. My old habits served me well. It was important to identify a positioning in the market for myself. Ralli Brothers—represented by my father and brother, Akbar—bought cotton from the large factories that were geared for the export market. I began to represent smaller ginny factories and address the local market, becoming a handling or commissioning agent interacting with Pakistani users and buyers of cotton. After all, I was not in competition or conflict with my father.

We were entering the mid-1960s. The initial euphoria of freedom had dissipated and Pakistanis had resumed their humdrum lives. The Quaid-e-Azam was with us for only a year, having died in September 1948 due to complications arising from tuberculosis. This was tragic—not only did the country lose its foremost leader but the incipient process of democracy was also rudely interrupted. We did not get the Constitution we deserved. From a sense of national purpose in 1947, politicians quickly reverted to groupism and factionalism, with spells of confusion and turmoil. This created a political and administrative vacuum that bureaucrats and, later, military generals sought to fill. As the line went, 'Once they [the bureaucrats and generals] entered, they never left.' They often gave themselves mandates—including economic and social sector policymaking—they were not suited for. The Quaid-e-Azam had visualized a Muslim nation but a secular state, where non-Muslim minorities would enjoy their rights. This was a nuanced vision that lesser men did not understand. Even in the 1950s and the 1960s, Karachi was a city of mosques, of course, but also had its temples, churches, even synagogues. There was a small Jewish community, and I have encountered Urdu-speaking Jews in London, those who were born in Pakistan but subsequently emigrated. Some ginny factories in Sindh were and are owned by Hindus. There was a well-respected Parsi community as well. In my travels to Balochistan, I encountered Hindus who spoke flawless Balochi. It was an interesting and diverse society but we could sense that things were changing. The biggest disappointment was that the government did not pay adequate attention to the economy, to infrastructure, to creating jobs, to educating people. Only that could sort out Pakistan's problems.

With democracy not taking off in Pakistan and civilian politicians not delivering on their promises to the masses, the time was ripe for strong military intervention. This came in October 1958, when General Ayub Khan led a coup and declared himself President. In 1960, he sought validation through an indirect referendum and won a handsome victory. A tall, strapping man and a popular soldier, Ayub Khan was actually welcomed by ordinary Pakistanis, since they were tired of political squabbling and yearned for good, decisive governance.

In the long run, it didn't help us and set the stage for repeated military interjections in our politics. In 1958, though, people were so tired of political intrigues that the coup seemed a relief. These issues didn't affect me directly as my business hardly required me to interact with the government or depend on orders or favours from its officials and ministers. Nevertheless, the greater currents of the day and the country did leave many of us anxious. Ayub Khan's tenure lasted till 1969, when ill health and political issues caused him to gradually hand over power to the army and then to General Yahya Khan. In retrospect, Ayub Khan's early years were not bad. To give him credit, he brought in economists and competent civil servants to devise and implement successive five-year plans. The Second Five-Year Plan (1960–65) and the Third Five-Year Plan (1965–70) emphasized industrial development and featured some sound proposals. Ayub Khan focused on economic growth and this phase constituted the only concentrated period—or at least the longest concentrated period—of economic strategizing in Pakistani history. Alas, the achievements fell short of expectations. Also, rather than continue on the lines Ayub Khan had thought of in the early 1960s, his successors imposed martial law, disempowered some notable technocrats and further constricted the space for politics and policy debate.

Admittedly, I am getting ahead of the story. At a personal level, I had nothing to do with Ayub Khan or any of the other national figures. I was busy with steel and cotton, with bailing hoops and yarn prices. Bit by bit, I rebuilt my capital and surpassed what I had been able to attain during my stint at SCC. The bad memories of Shamshuddin were behind me. As I grew older and settled into business, I gradually found time to meet my friends as well. Many of my mates from the Aga Khan Gymkhana used to complain that I had little time for them and was perennially busy. By the mid-1960s, I made it a point to redress this and socialize and interact with my friends at least once a week, usually late in the evening when the work for the day was done. I loved films, particularly Hollywood Westerns, and John Wayne was a personal favourite. We used to catch the last show at the movies and follow this up with dinner at a street eatery, wolfing down chicken tikkas and other delicacies. On holidays, we would play cricket. My fast-bowling skills were intact and I often bowled 25 overs in a day's cricket. This left my body aching and required the services of a masseur in the park, shortly after the game was over. It was all good fun.

In terms of business, Hasan Ali and Company—which was now my principal business vehicle—won a major export order in 1965 and sent 500 tonnes of cotton to the Soviet Union. Hasan Ali, of course, was my beloved brother. He had come back from London in 1963, after his wife completed an advanced degree in medicine, but was not the same man he had been before he left. He was clearly unwell and while we set up a company together—I did most of the work, to be honest, but desperately wanted

Hasan Ali to feel secure and satisfied—his physical and mental state did not allow him to perform to his potential. Sometime later, he developed an acute case of thrombosis (blood clotting), which remained untreated despite his wife being a doctor. His body was full of clots, and one of his legs turned blue and gangrenous. He was flown to London for treatment, but the leg had to be amputated. This negligence on the part of his wife was the last straw, and Hasan Ali divorced Laila as soon as he returned to Karachi. Later, further complications developed and he was rushed to London again, but couldn't be saved. A very popular man in Karachi and London, Hasan Ali died in 1974 at the age of forty-two. A year earlier, Zulfiqar Ali Bhutto had nationalized a whole host of businesses and crippled our cotton trade. That had broken Hasan Ali's spirit. By then, my other brother Akbar too had started helping me with my business. His Ralli Brothers operations had shut down in 1968.

To go back to 1965, the Soviet order was a big one for me and also signified a new business—bulk cotton exports as opposed to small domestic deals. Getting finance to execute the order was difficult. Banks were conservative in their lending. We were newcomers and too small for the large banks to trust us. Again, one had to be innovative. I offered a share of the contract to a bigger company and shared resources as well as profits with this company. In the end, the deal went through without a problem and my credibility was established. It was a valuable learning experience and gave me much confidence. In spite of sharing the surplus, I had made a reasonable profit from the venture and this got me thinking about the opportunities in cotton exports. There were not too many cotton exporters in Pakistan at that time. The risk and the complexity—getting good quality cotton, sorting out international trade regulations and permissions, guaranteeing delivery to and payment from a far-off country—scared potential players. This left the cotton export market free to a cabal of giants—Ralli Brothers, of course; Volkert Brothers (a Swiss concern); the group run by Parsi businessman Hakimuddin Hormozi; the Crescent Group; the Habib Group. Could a smaller, newer company fit in and do well? That was my challenge. The Soviet deal—500 tonnes or 4500 bales—gave me the courage to expand my horizons. I realized I would need to build a business on low margins, quick turnover and small establishment costs. These were the back-end values I sought to embed in my operations. To my buyers, my reputation, reliability and price would matter and determine whether repeat orders would be forthcoming.

The second consignment of cotton we sent was to North Korea and the third to China. We were beginning to build a name for ourselves and performing well in the very competitive cotton export trade. I have used the pronoun 'we' because it was my company that executed the orders and my brother helped me, at least notionally. In reality, I was running a one-man operation. In business, balance sheets and revenue statistics tell their own story. Yet, what a businessman wants is recognition from his peers and from the market. This is intangible and cannot be quantified in dollars or rupees. For me, it came one day in the mid-1960s when, seeing the surge in my cotton export business, a leading member of the Crescent Group said loudly and publicly, 'Just who are these *launda*s (boys)?' The big guns were beginning to notice us. The Crescent Group was one of the 'twenty-two families' that dominated Pakistan's economy in the 1960s. It was run by two brothers, Mohammed Amin and Mohammed Bashir, and their nephew Salim Altaf. These twenty-two families, the Fancy family among them, had a stranglehold on cotton and commodities exports, banking and insurance, gas distribution—nearly every aspect of economic life. They were ruined by Bhutto's nationalization drive in the early 1970s but their legacy and nomenclature lives on. The idea that the Pakistan economy is monopolized by a few elite families—the current expression is 'forty families'—has become a familiar one for journalists and writers.

Needless to say, I was not a member of any of the 'twenty-two families'; I had far humbler origins. I was not in their league, distant from their charmed circle, without an iota of the influence and political clout they enjoyed. I was a middle-class boy trying to make it. The cotton export market proved to be a gold mine for me. Orders didn't stop and we increased our sales year-on-year. China, Japan, Poland, Yugoslavia, Czechoslovakia, the Soviet Union: the telex kept buzzing, the telephone kept ringing. I was in the office from 8 a.m. till midnight. In the evening, I would go to the ships to see the cotton being loaded. On holidays, I tried to keep my social life going. I met a girl from the community and thought she was nice. I was in fact infatuated with her and sought my mother's permission to ask for her hand. My mother surprised me by saying no. The girl was from a family richer than ours and my mother felt she wouldn't be able to settle into our home and adjust to our living standards. I was hurt by the manner in which my mother explained it to me. 'Marry her if you want,' she said, 'but it will be difficult for me to adjust.' My mother was the pivot and head of the household. There was no question of disturbing that equilibrium and insulting her. I dropped the idea. A few months later, the girl got married to someone else and I couldn't help feeling morose. My mother walked up to me and asked me why I hadn't told her I felt so strongly. She would have agreed to the marriage, she said. I raised my hands and looked skyward—Allah must have had his reasons.

In 1968, my mother took very ill. She had been diagnosed with a life-threatening kidney ailment and was down to half her weight. We were very worried. One day, my mother turned to me and said, 'I want to see you married before I go. You are the last one not to be married.' My instant reaction was, 'Choose the girl you want. I will marry her without seeing her, just to fulfil your wish.' In part, this was an emotional response as I was worried about my mother's health and survival—with the blessings of God, she was able to recover and live for many more years—but the memory of my mother rejecting my choice also rankled. In the years since, I had channelled my hopes and energies and emotions into my work. I had no time to breathe, let alone to think of marriage. My mother consulted my sisters and nieces—some of them were adults themselves by then—and decided upon a girl whom I had never met. She was from an Ismaili family and my mother, having done her homework, felt she was an ideal choice. She was pointed out to me when she was in a group of ten or twelve girls. I nodded, unsure which one she was in that crowd. Following the wedding, we set off on our honeymoon to Egypt—where we saw the pyramids and the sights of Cairo—and then to Paris and London. It was my first trip abroad.

My marriage was to teach me a lot, and bring home some unpleasant and ironic truths. To be honest, we ran into problems and disagreements fairly soon. We were polar opposites and our individual cultures and values did not match, even though our families had commonalities. We had five children together but finally got divorced in 2011. In 1985, my mother had an honest chat with me and admitted to feeling guilty about my unhappy marriage. The girl she had so carefully chosen, after ticking off the parameters that seemed to matter to her, had been the wrong one for me. The girl I had wanted to marry had been turned down by her on the grounds that she didn't meet the criteria my mother felt appropriate for an ideal wife for me and for a daughter-in-law for our household. Destiny had bowled us this googly. 'Forgive me, Sadru,' my mother told me that day in 1985, 'I made a mistake. Why don't you marry again and find peace?' I brushed the thought aside. I had five children to bring up. I also had to work on my expanding business. Thinking of marriage and personal pleasures was the last thing I could afford.

4

COTTON KING

With the munificence of Allah, my hard work was paying off. In 1970, only five years after the first order from the Soviet Union, I was the number one exporter of cotton in Pakistan and had won the sobriquet 'King of Cotton'. In half a decade, I had overtaken the established names, some of them from the 'twenty-two families' and with literally centuries of wealth behind them. Inevitably, my success aroused jealousy. In 1970 itself, at one point, I had taken a long position on cotton futures—that is, bet on the price rising in the future. I was being a contrarian as many of the experienced hands in Karachi Cotton Association (KCA) had taken short positions. My rivals saw it as an opportunity to finish me once and for all. As such, even though the three-month cotton futures contract had been concluded, leading members of the KCA conspired to raise the deposit on contracts with retrospective effect. If I failed to pay the additional deposit, I would lose a vast sum and would not be able to honour my futures commitments either. I was in a tizzy and decided to challenge the circular that raised the deposit with retrospective effect. I went to the High Court of Sindh but it was closed for the summer months. During this 'vacation period', only a small 'vacation bench' functioned, rather than the full court. Heading the vacation bench was a senior judge who was close to the promoters of the Crescent Group, which had instigated the conspiracy against me. With an unsympathetic and even prejudiced judge, and the money power of the cotton establishment, many felt I was sunk. No senior commercial or civil lawyer would take on my case. Left with no other alternative, I had to appeal to Hayat Junejo, a distinguished criminal lawyer, to argue my case. Ranged against him was the well-known commercial lawyer Ramchandani Dingomal, assisted by his son Persi. It was a no-contest.

Very soon, my lawyer, an authority on criminal matters but lost in the wily by-lanes of commercial law, ran out of arguments and I ended up arguing my own case. The judge refused to strike down the circular or place a stay (suspension) on it. He admitted my petition and called for regular hearings, but insisted I had to pay the incremental deposit within twenty-four hours. I was in a quandary. I didn't have the money and my banking overdraft limits had been exhausted. I couldn't go to my regular bankers for more. Private moneylenders would not give me money, as the presumption was that this was the end of the road for me. I took a chance and went to the Karachi branch of the Bank of China. I had known the general manager (GM), a Chinese gentleman called K.L. Sung, and he was aware of my reputation. I explained my predicament. He took out a piece of paper—a blank paper, not one with my letterhead or company name and details or anything formal—and said, 'Write out an application right now.' Then he took my application and walked off. Fifteen minutes later, he returned with the pay order in favour of the 'Karachi Cotton Association'. It was a miracle—I couldn't believe my eyes. Subsequently, Sung was to become a close and dear friend. Armed with the pay order, I rushed to the KCA office. On the first floor, I ran into Qassim Mittha, chairman of the KCA. He smirked and mocked me, saying, '*Ab kahan jaaoge?* (Where will you go now?)' I was thirty-one and had a bit of a short fuse. 'You are an elderly man,' I said quietly. 'I respect you. If you had been my age, I would have thrown you off the balcony.' He stopped, stunned and a little frightened. I thrust the pay order into his hands and said, 'I am paying the deposit now.' He was shocked: 'You . . . you got the money?' 'Yes,' I said emphatically and walked off with a flourish. Then I turned back and shouted out, 'And I'm depositing it right now.' Having deposited the pay order, I called for delivery. This meant that those who had taken short positions would have to buy at whatever price the cotton was available and offer contracts of delivery to me. This created a crisis. The cotton market shut down for three days as many senior cotton traders were going to turn defaulters. On the third day, a delegation came to my house and sued for peace. We agreed to a compromise and the market reopened. That was the turning point. The power equation altered forever and the KCA did not play dirty with me again. As they say, 'The dogs bark, but the caravan moves on.'

The following year, 1971, saw other types of dogs at work—the dogs of war. It began with the East Pakistan crisis and a bitter and bloody power struggle between the two wings of Pakistan. India took full advantage and fuelled the fires of separatism among Bengali-speaking Pakistani Muslims. It provoked a conflict that eventually led to the creation of what is today Bangladesh. In December 1971, Pakistan and India went to war. Despite India's protestations that it was only engaged in humanitarian intervention in East Pakistan, the fact is that it was the aggressor in West Pakistan. I saw one of my city's landmarks, Karachi harbour, bombed by the Indian Navy. Indian Air Force planes also targeted Karachi. There were blackouts in the city and we had to sit at home in the dark. I found this suffocating and often took my car out for a short drive. My parents tried to stop me but I was insistent. I was fed up with the dark curtains and the candlelight. No invader was going to keep me bound indoors in my own city. Indian planes were flying overhead; I could see the bombs falling. The city was bombed extensively. Oil installations and military facilities were repeatedly attacked. At a roadside cafe, I would stop for tea. Nothing was said, nothing needed to be said. India's assault and cussed determination to weaken Pakistan's economic foundations was obvious. What had Karachi got to do with India's alleged sympathy for the Bangladesh cause?

The war of 1971 concluded with enormous unpleasantness. Pakistan lost territory. Many people in the former East Pakistan were massacred and many others came to West Pakistan as refugees. The bloodshed between Bengali and non-Bengali speaking people in the East, all of them Pakistanis and all of them Muslims, had taken place both before and after the war with India. It had demanded an enormous human cost. It is sobering to recall that Ismailis were not harmed after the breaking away of Bangladesh. Their charitable work had won them admiration and they were allowed safe passage. In the end, I suppose it is dignified behaviour that wins you respect, not just wealth. The war and its aftermath left me with searching questions. Was it worth it? Would it have been fine to live together, keep Pakistan united, even if it meant being ruled from Dhaka and having a Bengali-speaking prime minister (PM)? In a sense, we were (and still are) paying for the unfinished business of 1947 and for the unseemly hurry in which the British drew boundaries and left. They created conditions for mutual bitterness between Muslims and Hindus, and Pakistanis and Indians. They created conditions for an unresolved problem such as Kashmir, whose people have suffered oppression by the Indian Army for over six decades.

The conclusion of hostilities in 1971 also inaugurated the Bhutto era in Pakistani politics and brought Zulfiqar Ali Bhutto to the forefront of our public life. It was a period of confusion and economic turbulence, domestically and internationally. In 1973, my company lost an appreciable amount of money as a consequence of the oil shock and the dramatic rise in petroleum prices. This caused commodity prices to shoot up. Many ginny factories, which had committed to supplying cotton to me, did not deliver at the previously agreed rate. Taking advantage of the oil shock and the price rise, they asked for more. The problem was that I too had committed to selling cotton to my buyers in other countries at a certain price. Unlike the ginny factory owners, I was not going to renege on my promises. I would have to honour my contracts, even if it meant that my cost price was higher than my selling price. How would I cover the shortfall? After all, I had never defaulted on payments in my career. I decided to sell some property and real estate. Here again, fate took a fortunate turn. Sitting in my office one day, I had a walk-in visitor. He announced himself as a representative of the Louis Dreyfus Group, a French trading conglomerate. Borris Chapherd, as the man was called, had a supercilious air. He wanted to buy rice, he said, and was willing to place a single order of 14,000 tonnes. I called the GM of my grain department and asked him to make inquiries. We dealt in grain but for the local market, not yet having entered the export sector. I told Chapherd I would quote him a rate by the evening and invited him to dinner.

We dined at the trendy Maxim's restaurant in Clifton before I dropped him at the InterContinental Hotel, where he was staying. As he was getting out of the car, he asked me if I had a price. 'One hundred and thirty-five dollars per tonne FOB,' I said. FOB is an acronym for 'freight on board', meaning the buyer pays the freight. I had given myself a margin of 10 dollars per tonne for negotiations. Chapherd answered gruffly: 'You're expensive. I can get the same rice 10 dollars cheaper . . . but I accept the deal. Not because you're clever but because I know you will deliver . . . I have heard you are a man of your word.' By the time the rice was loaded on to the ship, the prevailing price had gone up to 160 dollars a tonne but I had made a commitment and there was no question of changing my mind. In any case, my cost price had been much lower. Being a street-smart Jew, Chapherd had done his homework and completed his due diligence before coming to my office. 'He had not studied my face,' as I later told a friend, 'he had studied my reputation and track record.'

That one transaction with Louis Dreyfus proved to be extremely profitable. It opened the door for me to cover my losses in cotton. Soon there was a queue of international buyers at my door, seeking rice. At this juncture, there was surplus rice in Pakistan because the main rice-eating region of the country—East Pakistan— had become another nation and the rice producers had lost that large market. The rice intended for East Pakistan was ready to be exported. We were not the only ones thinking on those lines; in fact, we were the last major company to come into the export trade. Even so, in just four months, I was Pakistan's top rice exporter, dealing in both types of rice found in Pakistan—the coarse rice grown in Sindh and Basmati grown in Punjab.

Shortly after this, I started exporting barley and maize as well. In 1974, I tied up with the Continental Grain Company (now ContiGroup) in New York, becoming its rice buyer and agent in Pakistan. I dealt with two executives from Continental, both of whom happened to be Jews with origins in Alexandria, Egypt. Rapael Tota and Myer Lisbona went on to become close friends. In the 1980s, I was in London when I heard that Lisbona, who had by then retired and settled in Rio de Janeiro, had passed away. He had invited me so often to Rio for the carnival but I had never been able to go; now I was travelling to the funeral of this loving, caring, father-like figure. Through my years of dealing with Continental, I always sold them grain at the pre-decided or contractual price, irrespective of whether market prices had changed in the interim. One year, there was a drought in Indonesia and Thailand and rice prices almost doubled in a matter of months. Many Pakistani exporters defaulted or threatened to default and demanded more money. I didn't. At one stage, I had pending shipments with Continental amounting to 58,000 tonnes of rice. I had agreed to sell at 235 dollars a tonne but the prevailing rate was 450 dollars a tonne. The difference of some 12 million dollars was a fortune. Tota and Lisbona were visiting Karachi during that period and I had taken them out to dinner. 'The market has shot up,' Lisbona began, 'and you may not be getting rice from the people you had ordered from. Should we consider revising the price?' I was visibly upset. 'Have I complained?' I asked. 'I treat you like a father figure but today you have hurt me. How can you even think of telling me to do something that is not right? My profit and loss is my business. My word is more important to me than money. I want to be able to look people in the eyes. That is my greatest profit.' Immediately, both the senior men apologized. I fulfilled my commitment to Continental to the last grain.

Meanwhile, Bhutto's government was making its presence felt. Bhutto was a good speaker, supremely self-assured, but also given to rhetorical flourishes and populism. He began to see, or projected himself as seeing, business and commerce as public enemies. In 1975, a problem arose between the government and me when the income tax law was changed for the previous year and the accounting year was suddenly transformed from 365 days to 557 days. It made no sense. In that period, I had lost money in the cotton trade but had made handsome gains in the rice trade. The post facto lengthening of the accounting year was engineered to damage me and increase my tax liability. Hasan Ali and Company—as my flagship company was still called—was the biggest loser and perhaps the sole reason for this bizarre, one-time change that was the brainchild of Mubashir Hassan, a scientist who had strangely been appointed finance minister in Bhutto's Pakistan People's Party (PPP) government. Once more, I took the issue to court and won the case. It is cited as a precedent in legal books to this day. Commenting on the astounding 557-day year in Pakistan, the Chief Justice of the Supreme

Court of Pakistan, Justice Yakub Ali Khan, had a direct question for S.A. Nusrat, appearing for the government: 'How can you do this? Has it ever happened in the history of the world?' I could have fudged numbers and earnings and bribed my way up the income tax department. That was probably the government's intention but I refused to succumb. I wanted to fight for my rights and for what was right. Thankfully, I succeeded.

Bhutto had become President in December 1971, just days after the war ended. In August 1973, he got redesignated as PM, being elected under a new Constitution. He was the first national leader I studiously avoided meeting though I had had a nodding acquaintance with the generals who preceded him and had friends in his PPP. My reason was simple enough: to Bhutto, his opinion was the last opinion. He didn't relish debate or discussion and was intolerant of dissent. I was used to speaking my mind and realized that if Bhutto felt I had crossed the line, he would put me on some negative list or a blacklist. I carried on with my business, away from the limelight. Instinctively, I didn't trust that man, with his advocacy of a socialism that I knew would end up throttling economic growth and empowering bribe-seeking public officials.

Between 1972 and 1974, Bhutto went on a reckless nationalization drive. He nationalized the steel and cement industries, banks and the rice and cotton mills.

He began by nationalizing thirty-two industrial units under ten categories, covering everything from iron and steel to electricity generation and distribution to oil and gas refineries. In early 1974, he invited major bankers and heads of insurance companies for a New Year's Day dinner at the State Bank building in Karachi and assured them: 'I will support you and help you grow and expand your business.' They left happy. A few hours later, he announced the nationalization of their banks. He was manipulative and untrustworthy—and he didn't understand economics. How else do you explain the government takeover of rice-husking factories, flour mills, vegetable oil manufacturers and cotton ginny units? He sought to control trade and industry through his loyal bureaucrats—who were not competent for the job—and pretended he was doing this in the name of the poor, to punish the rich. His outlandish finance minister, Mubashir Hassan, described businessmen not as wealth creators or assets but as 'robber barons'. Pakistan's economy is still paying for that leftward tilt in the early 1970s, which was entirely antithetical to the ethos of the country and of Muslim society.

What was most disappointing was Bhutto's murder of the education system. One fine day, he nationalized education and brought extremely well-run schools and colleges, the backbone of society, under government control. This jeopardized the future of the country and its coming generations. Western textbooks were removed or even sent back to the West and replaced by local books that were often shoddy. There was no incentive any more to set up schools or colleges. Astonishingly, this came from a man who had been sent by his father to the best of schools and then to the University of California, Berkeley, and Oxford University. One day, Bhutto ran into his old senior Ramchandani Dingomal, a well-known commercial lawyer in whose firm (Dingomal and Company) Bhutto had begun his legal career. The story, related to me by Dingomal's son Persi—who now lives in Bombay—is telling. 'I say, Zulfi,' the senior Dingomal said, 'you have gone and nationalized education. Why?' Bhutto laughed, 'Relax, your children and my children are not going to be studying here in Pakistan anyway, are they?'

5

A TASTE OF HOSPITALITY

It was in 1973 that the cotton and rice trades were nationalized. I was in Toronto on a business visit when I received a call from my brother Hasan Ali. He sounded panicky and I was worried there was bad news on the family front. He told me about the nationalization. It was a blow but I realized at once that, more than Hasan Ali and me, the people who worked for us would be in a predicament. They were ordinary employees, people who had known nothing but the rice and cotton trade. If they lost their jobs, they would be on the streets, for they had been trained for no other line of business. In any case, with more and more companies coming under state control, dignified and professional managers and workers would not find it easy to beg bureaucrats for jobs. One of the first things I told Hasan Ali from Toronto was that on no account was there to be any retrenchment at our companies and that everybody had to be assured of job security. 'Protect everybody's salaries till I come back,' I said. 'Everything must go on as normal. Let me return, we will seek new avenues.'

I had an inkling of where these new opportunities lay, but what had been just the germ of an idea acquired urgency after the nationalization spree. For some time, I had been mulling over the idea of setting up a hotel. I felt Pakistan was ready to develop a mature leisure economy and attract more tourists. For this, it needed good hotels. I was familiar with hotels and their culture. I had even gone to discotheques—admittedly more out of curiosity than to dance wildly. I liked eating out, especially on Thursday evenings (Friday being the Muslim day for prayer and rest) and on Saturday evenings (Sunday being the conventional weekend). That apart, I liked the excitement of a start-up, of a new challenge, of learning a new business. Cotton and rice exports, though rewarding and lucrative, had become boring and predictable for me. I knew them like the back of my hand. On the flight back from Toronto, I began crystallizing the hotel idea and wrote notes on some sheets of paper that I borrowed from the air hostess.

I already owned a piece of land in Karachi's Sadar area that I had bought in a distress sale the previous year.

This was prime real estate, in the heart of the city. I felt it was suitable for a hotel. In that period, following the nationalization spurt, many big tycoons gave up on Pakistan, sold their assets and either exited business or left the country altogether. I had no such intention—this was my country and I was going to stay put. Instead, I began investing even more in Pakistan, hoping for better times. That is how I came to acquire not just the Sadar area plot but several other assets as well. Take the properties of the Fancy family. Their steel mill was nationalized, as was Karachi Gas, which they ran. The government took over Commerce Bank and the New Jubilee Insurance Company, also part of the Fancy Group. The Fancy family was rattled. Their Quetta Textile Mill in Sindh had not been nationalized but they were now tending towards selling it, along with the small equity that they retained in some other companies, and several pieces of property.

These events set off the decline of the Fancy family and left me with bittersweet memories. I had come to know the family in a variety of phases, having worked with them as well as having had differences of opinion with them. As the reader may recall, I began my independent business career as a sales agent for the Steel Corporation of Pakistan, owned by the Fancy family, and sold bailing hoops the company manufactured. During that period I began to meet Shaukat Fancy, son of the family patriarch, Amir Ali

Fancy. Shaukat Fancy was a name to be reckoned with. As the man in charge of the sales department, he had to sign the delivery order. I was often made to wait for an hour or two outside his office. The social hierarchy was obvious.

In the course of our professional acquaintance, Shaukat Fancy came to hear of my reputation as an active sportsman and a regular at the Aga Khan Gymkhana. This was a well-known social and sporting institution, located inside a historic building in the heart of Karachi. It was dominated by happy-go-lucky sportsmen, many of whom were my friends. Shaukat Fancy approached me and asked for help to become a member of the Gymkhana and make a few of his friends members as well. I was happy to help. A few months later, he told me he and a few friends wanted to serve on the managing committee of the Gymkhana. I broached the subject with those who ran the place. They were sceptical. This was an easy-going committee, packed with sportsmen. Did they really need high-profile business tycoons and bankers? Again I used my persuasive skills and argued that bringing the city's social and economic elite into the managing committee would do no harm. In time, Shaukat Fancy became secretary of the Gymkhana and some of his friends were elected to the managing committee.

A year passed. One evening Shaukat Fancy asked to meet me and said he would like to replace Shaukat Macklai as president of the Gymkhana. I was aghast. Macklai was a genial man. Besides, he had just lost his wife in a plane crash in Cairo. He had been lucky to survive and still walked with a limp due to the injuries sustained in the crash. To ease him out of the Gymkhana's presidency seemed cruel. Nevertheless, I promised to sleep over the proposal and get back to Shaukat Fancy the following day. In the interim, I consulted a few friends and they too were shocked. I returned to Shaukat Fancy and asked a leading question: 'What will your role be?' He was quick to reply: 'I will continue as secretary. My cousin Abdul will become president.'

The game was obvious. The Fancy family would take over the Gymkhana. I told him I couldn't back his plan. He offered me inducements. 'We have substantial business interests in East Pakistan,' he said, 'supplying bailing hoops to jute mills. I will make you the sales agent and provide some financial support as well.' I was unmoved. Then he began talking of his father being a powerful person in the Ismaili community and in Karachi. I was adamant, saying I could not compromise on principles. At this, Shaukat Fancy banged his fist on the table and exclaimed, 'I am not requesting you. I am *asking* you . . .' I sat still. Then I got up, chose my words carefully and said, 'I don't have a price tag.' Walking away, I looked back from the door to add, 'I will see you on the day of the election.' As I exited, I knew my business relationship with the Fancy family was over.

Meanwhile, there was an election to be won. I got my friends to prepare for the contest. We went through the voters' list. Some members who were likely to vote for us were in default of fees and I paid for them, using my own money, to ensure they could vote. The Fancy family put all its resources into the contest. The degree of lobbying was unimaginable. Lavish parties were thrown to solicit support. Sometimes it seemed overwhelming for me and my friends. What was happening to our beloved Gymkhana? Was it becoming a plaything for the rich and famous? I was heartened when a member who had attended one of the Fancy parties said to me, 'My vote is yours. I will not betray you . . . But let me enjoy myself at these parties!' My confidence grew as the election approached.

When the votes were counted, the Fancy faction lost all the posts. They were routed. As a dejected Shaukat Fancy got into his limousine, I was wheeling out my bicycle. One of my friends, agitated and excited by the evening's events, grabbed Shaukat Fancy by the collar. I stopped him, saying, 'Don't dirty your hands.' Turning to Shaukat Fancy, I said, 'Shaukat, we are small people but we have character . . .' Shaukat Fancy stormed off. That was the end of his association with the Gymkhana.

Even so, I now had a determined enemy. The vengeance of the Fancy family came in 1968, a month before my daughter Nadia was born. One day, I was in a meeting with Zafar Minhaz, GM of the National Bank of Pakistan, when I received a phone call. I was told one of the warehouses where I stored cotton—by this time I had entered the cotton export trade—had caught fire. I rushed to the warehouse, reaching at about noon. The bales were on fire. As the fire brigade arrived, I made attempts to sequester and remove the bales that had so far escaped the flames. In all, 4000 bales had been damaged; they were part of a consignment meant to be sent to Yugoslavia. I approached the New Jubilee Insurance Company with a provisional claim of Rs 2.8 million. New Jubilee Insurance was owned by the Fancy family. It was managed by Mehmood Sabzalli, a Fancy loyalist.

The fire was unfortunate but such accidents happen in business. As was my wont, I shrugged it off and moved on. A few weeks later, I was summoned by the Martial Law Tribunal that had been assigned by Lieutenant General Riaz Hussain, the local military administrator, to investigate the fire. Three officers, one from each wing of the military and with little knowledge of commerce, began to interrogate me and ask ridiculous questions. From the outset they were trying to build a case of insurance fraud. I protested and presented my side of the story, but they were not convinced. One evening, at six o'clock, the Tribunal sent the police to my house to arrest me. An ordeal began. For forty days, I was kept in solitary confinement in Karachi's Haji Camp. My wife was expecting Nadia. Only she and my parents were allowed to see me, for no more than an hour a week. The food at the camp was inedible and my health suffered. What hurt most was to see my heavily pregnant wife and ageing parents make strenuous efforts to visit me. My parents were simple people. To watch me being treated like a criminal moved them to tears.

The Tribunal continued to question me. I was asked why I went to the warehouse when I did, how many bales I removed and saved from the blaze, and so on. The provisional insurance claim—it was, as would be obvious, provisional and liable to changes when more information and data became available—was challenged. Finally, it was decided that the provisional claim had been overstated by Rs 28,000 (or 1 per cent). The charges of fraud were not sustainable and I was released. Later I discovered that the Fancy family had instigated this so-called investigation.

Imagine the twists and turns of life: when the Bhutto nationalization spree started and the Fancy Group went into a state of panic, one of the companies whose shares I bought was New Jubilee Insurance. It closed a chapter for me and came to represent the diminishing fortunes of the once-formidable Fancy family.

Other people who had lost their business empires to nationalization and to Bhutto's government were equally keen to sell what remained of their assets. Given the pessimism, there were very few buyers. Ever the contrarian, I bet on a different future and put my money into several such assets that were up for sale. Soon I found myself with a textile mill, a cinema theatre and many pieces of property in Karachi.

The purchase that obsessed me immediately was the land in the Sadar area. I needed permission to build a hotel. The Bhutto government put forward a strange condition. There was no decent hotel in Islamabad, then emerging as Pakistan's capital. The government would grant me permission for a hotel in Karachi only if I agreed to build a hotel in Islamabad as well. Obviously, we were talking of five-star hotels, which required enormous capital. The condition doubled my fund requirement. Government bureaucrats apart, there were other obstacles. I was clear I wanted to run the hotel. I was ready to take the franchise of an international chain and learn from its expertise, but I was not willing to simply hand over management rights to an external hotel company and live off a small share of profits. I sought to enter the hospitality industry, not just earn rent from a building. International chains were not agreeable to this. Since there was a shortage of big hotels in Pakistan, particularly in its leading commercial city, Karachi, other entrepreneurs too had started hotel projects. They were fine with eschewing the franchise model and simply signing management contracts with the big chains. Sheraton signed up for the Ganjee family's hotel project. Hyatt Regency joined hands with Darayus Minwalla. Hilton sealed a deal with Dinshaw Avari and his company. I was left looking for a suitable international hotel chain as a partner, as well as for a dynamic and honest chief executive for the upcoming hotels. This would be the key person, working with me to build and get the hotel projects off the ground, to actually implement my plans.

I found the right person in the late S.M. Aslam. He was an engineer who used to work for the Fancy Group but, after nationalization, as the Fancy companies came under pressure, Aslam was looking for new openings. He agreed to take up the challenge of helping me build the hotels. Still unsure of my credentials and of the viability of a new hotel in Karachi, he drew up a rigorous agreement, with several terms and conditions, and brought it to me typed on a stamp paper. He gave it to me to read and offer my comments. To his surprise and shock, I signed it and handed it back in a jiffy. 'But you haven't read it,' he exclaimed. 'I have given you a major project, my biggest project, to implement,' I said. 'I'm entrusting you with all of that. I don't need to read contracts and this clause or that clause.' Aslam was moved. A tough, straightforward professional, he never let me down. Together we set out to look for an international partner. In 1974, I wrote to Holiday Inn for a franchise and was invited to its regional office in Hong Kong. The regional chief was a genial but plain-speaking German called Rudi Koppen. Early in our meeting, I told him I wanted the Holiday Inn franchise for all of Pakistan. 'You are building one hotel,' he said, 'and you want the franchise rights for the whole country?' I insisted I had plans to grow; besides, the hotel in Islamabad was also coming up. He agreed to two franchises for the hotels in Islamabad and Karachi, with the option of taking the franchise into the rest of Pakistan.

Being new to the hotel business, I decided to study and understand the Holiday Inn concept and visit its hotels in different cities of the world. Since we were in Hong Kong, I sought a meeting with the architects of the local Holiday Inn. Jackson Wong and his firm, Wong Yong Associates, had designed and built Holiday Inn hotels in Hong Kong and Singapore. Coincidentally, the owner of the Hong Kong hotel was Hari Leela, a Sindhi with roots in Karachi, who had migrated to Hong Kong in the 1950s. We hit it off and Leela made me an offer: 'Let's join hands and build and run hotels in Hong Kong and South East Asia.' It was a tempting offer, as the economies of the Asia-Pacific region were at the beginning of what was to become a sustained boom. Nevertheless, I wasn't interested. My quest was to build quality hotels in Pakistan. Leela understood my sentiments and wished me luck. He gave me good advice on the hotel business and clarified my doubts. Having signed an agreement with Wong Yong Associates, Aslam and I went to stay at and study the Holiday Inn in Singapore, a big property on Orchard Road, the main shopping and leisure destination in the city. In 1974, though, Singapore was still a small city, not the glitzy metropolis it has now become. Of course, it was already far ahead of many of its South East Asian peers, as the socio-economic transformation triggered by its leader, the venerable Lee Kuan Yew, was becoming evident.

Having finalized the franchise and architect, I flew back to Karachi and waited for Rudi Koppen and Jackson Wong to arrive. We took them to the proposed site of the hotel and, almost at once, Wong said it was too small for the scale and size I had in mind. We needed to look for an alternative. Then we flew to Islamabad, where I had committed to building a hotel. Here the government gave me the liberty of choosing a plot. Islamabad was a new city, emerging out of fields and open spaces. It was not an organically evolved city like Karachi, which had few free areas in its busiest parts. In Islamabad in the 1970s, land was aplenty. As luck would have it, we got an excellent plot, with a view of the verdant Margalla Hills that lie just north of Islamabad. The site couldn't have been better and we were all very happy. In Karachi, too, I asked the government to sell me some land for my hotel project. Again, the Almighty showered His blessings and I got access to a sizeable plot overlooking Frere Hall Garden (now Bagh-e-Jinnah, a sixteen-acre landmark) near the US Embassy. Both pieces of land, in Karachi and Islamabad, were about 18,000 square yards in area, enough for hotels of the type we were envisioning. Both projects started up simultaneously. Though built at the same time, the design, underlying theme and architectural conceptualization of the hotels were entirely different. What was common was that both hotels were to be built in two phases. My one condition was that when the hotels expanded, as custom picked up, the two phases should not stand apart but should merge into each other and look like a composite property. Of the hotel projects that started in that period, ours was the last to get down to construction. Yet, we worked hard and Aslam in particular spent long hours at the two sites, travelling from one city to the other. In twenty months, the Holiday Inn was ready and phase one of the hotel opened in 1978. This hotel is now the Islamabad Marriott.

By 1978, Bhutto had been ousted. You may wonder why I mention this in the midst of a story on hotel construction. The sad fact is, since politics and business are linked and enmeshed in Pakistan, any changes in the federal government, any coups, any power games impacted my hotel plans as well. In his final months in office—before he was removed in a coup in July 1977—Bhutto and his government had been urging us to finish the Islamabad hotel. Bhutto saw it as a showpiece of the capital and a world-class facility to host international dignitaries. He was recognizing the virtues of tourism. He was also beginning to regret nationalization and actually 'denationalized' some husking mills and ginny factories. Of course, he couldn't go very fast or very far because that would have amounted to admitting his ill-conceived socialism and his flawed nationalization binge—and no politician, certainly not Zulfiqar Ali Bhutto, likes to be proved wrong. Had he stayed on, would he have privatized many more companies? It is an intriguing question and I don't have a clear answer.

Till his last days in government, Bhutto continued to send ambiguous signals. When he was pushed by religious parties to ban alcohol consumption and prohibit horse-racing, or to declare Friday the weekly holiday, he compromised, notwithstanding his own Westernized habits. As early as 1974, he succumbed to demands made by religious conservatives and declared the small Ahmadiyya community as 'non-Muslim'. He was sowing seeds that others were to reap, notably his successor, General Zia-ul-Haq. In 1977, General Zia took over from Bhutto, imprisoning our PM and declaring himself the Chief Martial Law Administrator. A year later, Zia assumed the post of President of Pakistan. By then, it was apparent that he had brought in a new culture. He had no taste for hotels or for tourism. He felt the ongoing hotel projects were laundering money on behalf of Bhutto. He began investigating Bhutto's alleged financial interest in these projects. At the Hilton, Avari, one of Pakistan's most famous Parsis, quickly made friends with Zia, assured him of his support, and continued as before. Other projects were not so lucky. Since the banks had been nationalized by Bhutto, they were now under government control and Zia's men ran them. The banks began refusing credit for some hotel projects, including the Karachi Holiday Inn (now a Marriott). I had to tap into my own resources and drain my other businesses of cash to complete the Karachi hotel, which was meant to also house shops for big retailers. Rather than wait for this rental income, I approached prospective tenants and asked for large deposits that could be offset against rents when the hotel was finished. This eased my cash flow problems. I also began cutting costs, without compromising safety and quality, busying myself in the nitty-gritty of construction. As a result, I built both hotels at about half the cost of my competitors.

When the hotels opened, my loans for both hotels together amounted to 3 million dollars. In contrast, the Sheraton, which opened in Karachi in 1982, paid 3 million dollars in consultancy fees alone. This was an avoidable indulgence and, when I first heard about it, I just shook my head. In other matters too, I played with a straight bat. Hotel promoters had been given an import licence to bring in bathroom and bedroom fittings, air conditioning and lighting equipment, and elevators—which were not made in Pakistan—from overseas. Some other hotel promoters of the time brought in more items than they needed and sold the surplus on the black market, to wealthy Pakistanis. This gave them extra income. I did nothing of the sort; I was not interested in making loose change through such crooked, low-level practices. The Karachi Holiday Inn was inaugurated by my mother on 21 March 1981. It was Navroz, the traditional Iranian New Year and an auspicious occasion for Ismailis with origins in Iran. With my mother leading us in prayer, we opened the coffee shop, the banquet hall and one floor of guestrooms. We were hopeful of success but unsure. By end-1981, however, our fears had been put to rest. The hotel was doing so well and generating so much revenue that we had enough to spare to complete the other floors and finish the first phase as envisaged. I took great pleasure in telling the banks they did not have to disburse more money to us and that we didn't need their cash.

There was a history to my altercation with the banks. In February 1981, a month before the Karachi hotel began

taking in guests, I was summoned by the president of the
Banking Council of Pakistan. The presidents and chairs
of all the nationalized banks were present. I was told fresh
conditions were being imposed before releasing funds—the
undisbursed part of the agreed loan—to help complete the
hotel. I was told they didn't trust me and would give the
money directly to the contractors, painters, carpenters,
suppliers—not to me. Obviously, payments would be
delayed, angering my contractors and other vendors, who
would have wanted to continue with me as the customer
and single point of bill clearance and payment. To add to
that, a leading businessman, one who had never defaulted
on his loans and taxes, was being told that his long-standing
bankers no longer believed him. It was insulting and I was
fuming. 'Have you called me here to bank or beg?' I asked.
'It is better for me to stand outside the mosque rather than
sit here before you. I don't want your loan. Keep your
loan. After a month, I will open the hotel.' I stormed out.
As soon as I reached my office, I got telephone calls from
Aziz Sakrani, president of Muslim Commercial Bank, and
Qasim Parekh, chief of Habib Bank. 'In my entire life, I
have never heard the words you used today,' Sakrani said.
'People beg for money. You kicked it away!' Parekh was
more colloquial: '*Tumne hamaari dukaan phaad di* (You tore
apart our business). People come shivering to us but you
looked us in the eye.'

The Banking Council had tried to blackmail me at a critical stage, when the hotel was all but ready and only the proverbial last mile was left. The finishing touches were under way and we were preparing to pay our contractors and vendors. To have capital drying up right then was potentially catastrophic. Again, I drew upon my own resources and those of generous well-wishers. I wasn't going to let bumptious bank officials and Zia's government have the last laugh. In a month, the hotel was functional. Three years earlier, when the Islamabad Marriott had been completed, I had gone in for what is called a soft launch, without a grand inauguration. A big event would inevitably have involved Zia, then the Chief Martial Law Administrator. I wanted to avoid him and avoid giving my hotel a political colour. The February 1981 Banking Council experience told me I had been right about the man.

My first interaction with Zia after he took over the country had been on 22 February 1978. I had been invited to the house of Lieutenant General Habibullah Khan Khattak. A retired army officer, General Habibullah was well known in business circles and served as a federal minister during the Zia years. That day he was hosting a dinner for the visiting deputy PM of Romania. There were about twenty to twenty-five guests, and General Zia too made an appearance. Those were the first days of his tenure and both he and the other guests were sussing out each other.

Many critics of the Bhutto regime were present and permitting themselves a degree of casualness. General Habibullah himself had been imprisoned by Bhutto, since he was considered close to Ayub Khan. One of the guests was Ardeshir Cowasjee, part of a prominent Parsi family of Karachi, whose large shipping company had been nationalized by Bhutto. The outspoken Cowasjee— later a popular newspaper columnist before passing away in 2012—had been sent to jail by Bhutto in what was considered a whimsical and authoritarian act. At the party, Cowasjee took things to an extreme by asking General Zia, 'Where is my bottle of champagne?' Zia's reputation as a conservative Muslim who avoided alcohol was no secret, and this was perhaps not on. I was watching the interaction as a silent spectator. How would the general react? Would he laugh it off as a joke? Would he shrug his shoulders and change the subject or move to the next person? Instead, I saw blood in Zia's eyes—he was angry. I wanted to judge Zia for myself. I introduced myself to him as he was having dinner. I gave him what I call my direct eye-contact test—looking straight into a person's eyes. Does he look right back at you, does he shift his gaze? In my experience, whatever the other person does is revealing. The eyes convey a message. Zia's eyes conveyed cunning and intolerance. I came away feeling uncomfortable. This was my country's new self-appointed guardian. How good would or could he be for Pakistan?

A month later, I met the general again. Zia was visiting Karachi and a minister in the Sindh government had hosted a dinner in his honour. This time, he was accompanied by his senior advisers and surrounded by cronies, flatterers, favour-seekers. I went up and greeted him, hoping to end our conversation there. However, he stopped me and asked a question: 'So, what news?' I could have answered that in many different ways but, as always, my inner feelings came out. 'News?' I began . . . 'No news . . . Mr Bhutto ruined the economy and you are rewarding the same set of bureaucrats.' The reference was a general one but could have been construed as a dig at some of the people around him at the party. Zia froze, but I was just starting. 'Mr Bhutto didn't establish a Potato Corporation of Pakistan, that's about it . . . Only that needed to be done. Switch on the TV and all you see are mullahs . . . Please focus on the economy—we are sunk otherwise. Get rid of these bureaucrats from the corporations. Corruption is multiplying, pilferage and theft are rampant. Please visit the warehouse of the Cotton Corporation, trucks are stealing stocks through the night.' Zia said nothing. After a few seconds of delicate silence, he turned to the person next to him and said, 'Let's eat.'

I had been brushed aside. His anger was palpable. He was not used to being told home truths.

Retribution was swift. Early the following morning, at eight, I got a call from Noor Leghari, chief of the Intelligence Bureau in Karachi. Leghari was a friend but I could tell he was groping for words and a bit uncomfortable. I asked him to speak up. Finally he did: 'Sadru bhai, there is a message from General Zia. Please don't speak to him or even bother wishing him socially. You are forbidden from doing so.' I exploded: '*Bhaad mein jao* (Go to hell) . . . And please convey this to General Zia.' I had been declared persona non grata. Within a week, not just me but the entire family had been put on the Exit Control List—even my father who had died over a year earlier, on 14 May 1977. I couldn't leave the country and oppressive inquiries began into the affairs of my company and my financial records. Every aspect of my life was under scrutiny. Consider the irony. I was trying to build hotels and enhance Pakistan's reputation for hospitality—and a dictatorial government was bent upon making Pakistan itself inhospitable for me.

6

A FUGITIVE AT HOME

Investigations against me and against the Hashoo Group were launched in full earnest. The Martial Law Administrator of Karachi assigned the inquiry to Brigadier Tajamul Hussain, a man who seemed to have a vindictive streak. Almost every day, I was summoned by Hussain to the Martial Law Summary Court. His colleagues and he were looking to put a noose around my neck but lacked clinching evidence. Actually they lacked any evidence at all, as the cases against me collapsed in the course of time. Yet, whenever I was called, they repeated the same question with unrelenting regularity: 'Is Zulfiqar Ali Bhutto your secret partner?' They refused to believe me when I said I had never even met Bhutto, let alone collaborated with him.

'Why didn't you meet him?' Brigadier Hussain asked, turning his assumption on its head.

'Why should I have? I had no need to,' I said.

'But he gave you such a prized plot to build a hotel.'

'I had my own plot of land in Karachi but needed a better and bigger one. In Islamabad, the plot was allotted to me by the government because it wanted me to build a hotel. It was felt that the new capital needed a good hotel. If you so desire, please take the plot back . . .'

'All that is fine, but tell us what favours Mr Bhutto did for you?'

'I have never asked for a favour of anybody but Allah. And Mr Bhutto nearly ruined me by nationalizing the cotton trade one fine day . . . If he has done me a favour, show me where and how. I will answer it at once.'

My work and professional obligations began to suffer. Rather than attend office and participate in business meetings, I found myself being harassed by a brigadier who knew little of commerce and accountancy, and simply did not understand what I did for a living. He was bent upon making life difficult for me. I used to be called to the Summary Court and often made to wait several hours, before being asked the same questions to which I gave the same answers. Finally, despite Hussain's dogged efforts, the inquiry team came to the conclusion that I had done nothing wrong. From the Central Board of Revenue to the income tax authorities, one by one, government departments were to clear me and my companies of all charges and the pressure was to ease. On my part, I continued to criticize Zia for what I felt were misplaced socio-economic policies.

Discerning readers may detect a contradiction here. Earlier in the book I had said that I avoided speaking to Bhutto as I did not want to make an enemy of him and realized he was a man who took dissent personally. Yet, I was willing to speak up against Zia. Why? What was the difference? To be honest, I had the courage to speak out against Zia and criticize him as a matter of course because I knew that despite his authority and overwhelming powers, he was constrained by an institution: the army. If he did something that was absolutely outrageous and discriminatory and violated morality, other generals and corps commanders, even former generals who had a voice and certain influence in Pakistani society—and whose counsel Zia couldn't easily brush aside—would intervene and protest. In contrast, in his heyday in the early 1970s, Bhutto was answerable to none. His sway over the masses and his populist rhetoric had made him heady with power. Though he had the outward appearances of a civil and democratic leader, in my opinion he was thoroughly dictatorial, even despotic. He sent people to prison at random, without legal justification.

The tragedy of Pakistan is that even civilian politicians have sought to become dictators here. On the other hand, military dictators have sought democratic validation but on their own terms, without becoming genuine democrats. This paradox has troubled Pakistan almost since its birth and ended up constricting space for genuine democratic politics. Military dictators are not believers in democracy in the first place, and civilian leaders end up trying to sabotage it for their own ends. There is use, misuse and abuse of power by both types of leaders. Ironically though, as I explained, structured disagreement is possible within the institutional framework of the army. Alternative points of view can be argued for and alternative power sources can be appealed to, at least behind closed doors. This was possible with the army under Zia. It was not possible with Bhutto because he was the undisputed leader of the PPP and his cabinet comprised sycophants. On my part, I have always believed that business is not just about profit and loss and commercial transactions. It cannot be divorced or sequestered from the ethical underpinnings and challenges of the society within which it exists. I had a commitment to my companies, my employees and my clients. I had an even greater commitment to Pakistan. This country had given so much to me and to successive generations of my family; I was duty-bound to help build it as an economy, a society and a polity. If this meant protesting when a military ruler took a wrong turn, so be it. Many of my businessmen friends didn't see my point. 'Why are you doing it Sadru?' I was asked so often. 'You are a businessman, mind your own business. You can't take on everybody.' My answer was constant: 'This is my country, my *sarzameen* [native land] . . . I have an obligation to it. I must say what I believe is right. If the general does something incorrect and we too keep quiet like cowards, how does it help? Two wrongs don't make a right.'

What was most revolting was the hypocrisy of Zia's favourites and of some of those who grew rich and powerful by keeping him happy. In the Quran, I had been taught as a young boy, hypocrisy was equated with 'eating the meat of a dead brother', on par with cannibalism. In Pakistan, by the early 1980s, hypocrisy was becoming the national pastime. By 1985, disaffection against the Zia administration was beginning to reach critical proportions.

There was also criticism from the international community. Despite being a favourite of the Americans, Zia was taunted for having promised a quick return to democracy and early elections in 1977 but delivering nothing. It had been eight years since he had taken charge in that coup. There was still no sign of reverting to democratic politics or of Zia relinquishing charge. In December 1984, Zia held a referendum. He was the only candidate and people were given the right to elect or reject him as President. It was not clear what would happen if they rejected him. There was no other candidate and nobody seriously expected Zia would go quietly into the sunset. The referendum was a travesty—10 per cent of Pakistan's adult citizens voted and Zia won a 95 per cent majority.

Two months later, he permitted parliamentary elections without allowing parties to put up candidates or use party symbols. This led to Mohammad Khan Junejo, an acolyte of General Zia and descendant of a feudal family in Sindh, becoming PM. Junejo appeared simple and docile in public but that exterior masked a corrupt and petty mentality. As a senior politician, Junejo had imported a car, a Mercedes, into Pakistan using forged documents. One day, his secretary, Iqbal Junejo, telephoned me and requested me to buy the car. I was perplexed. I didn't need a car, I said, and I didn't drive a Mercedes anyway. 'But please buy it,' Iqbal said. 'Mr Junejo will be very happy. He will be glad if you bought it.' I asked to see the car and the import documents. On perusing them, I realized they were forgeries. The car had come in as part of a smuggling racket, cheating the exchequer of import duties. Junejo was trying to make a tidy profit by using his political clout to sell it locally. What had Pakistan done to deserve such person as PM? General Zia was equally problematic. He banned Indian films from being released commercially and refused to allow ordinary citizens to watch them. Then, in the privacy of his house, he watched these films himself. I know this for a fact because common friends were invited to these private screenings.

Zia's strength was his nose for survival. Even though he was a soldier, he had a politician's mind for conspiracy and guile, which had helped him attain office in the first place. He made a fool of Bhutto who appointed him Chief of Army Staff after superseding eleven generals, some of them more deserving than Zia. How Zia ingratiated himself to Bhutto is a saga worth recounting. He was the judge in the court martial that followed the Attock Conspiracy, where some senior military officers were accused of plotting a coup against the Bhutto government. Zia held the accused officers to be guilty and sentenced them to death. The sentence was extremely harsh and Bhutto himself was forced to call for moderation. Finally, a lighter sentence was given but Zia had impressed Bhutto by his willingness to hand out a death sentence to anybody who threatened Bhutto's government. When the two men met, Zia would bow his head and speak politely and humbly, as if addressing an emperor or spiritual leader. As a result, Bhutto grew confident that Zia was loyal to him and very malleable. He would never have imagined his hand-picked army chief was preparing to become his hangman and would ultimately oversee his execution in April 1979.

What changed Zia's luck was the Soviet invasion of Afghanistan in December 1979. It changed the atmosphere in Pakistan and transformed the American attitude towards Zia. From the dictator who had sent Bhutto to the gallows, he was now viewed as a frontline ally in the Cold War. In Pakistan itself, the Afghan jihad began to be promoted by Zia. Muslims from many countries, from good, even wealthy families, were encouraged to come to Pakistan and make it a base for battling the Soviet army and liberating Afghanistan. Zia balanced his new popularity in London and Washington DC by mobilizing religious forces and extremists in Pakistan, to help the mujahideen in Afghanistan and to give himself a political constituency at home. Pakistan became the station for millions of refugees from Afghanistan, some of them turning to arms. All this was to have long-term implications for Pakistan and for the world but were not obvious in the 1980s. Today, they are recognized as part of Zia's legacy. The very people in the West who praised and helped him thirty years ago now demonize him. In many respects, they are even more hypocritical than he was, but that's another matter.

I had nothing to do with international politics of course and was continuing to seek emerging business opportunities. I formed a JV with Philip Morris, the tobacco giant, and became 40 per cent owner of its Pakistani subsidiary, Premier Tobacco. Again, this was a new field for me and I walked in without realizing what I was getting into. Existing players in the tobacco business in Pakistan, some of whom participated in borderline organized crime, were shaken up. It was like I had awakened the crocodiles. I became the victim of a whisper campaign and of intense lobbying by corporate rivals.

Zia was told I was funding the PPP, Bhutto's party, which was headed after his death by his daughter, Benazir Bhutto. Benazir had been placed under arrest by Zia and subsequently sent into exile in London. In 1986, she returned to Pakistan and was welcomed by large crowds. This made Zia nervous. I didn't know Benazir at all and was certainly not paying money to the PPP. Even so, within weeks of Benazir's return, the military-backed regime raided my house and arrested me, charging me with giving 25 lakh rupees in political funds to her and to the PPP and allegedly supporting attempts to overthrow the government. This was nonsense. I was accused of paying Benazir through my cousin Pyar Ali Allana, a prominent member of the PPP. In 1985, Ghulam Ali Allana had died after a distinguished career as a public servant and scholar. He had left some money in a trust and put me in charge. From this trust fund, I was meant to give small sums of money periodically to, among others, Pyar Ali, son of Ghulam Ali Allana. This was misrepresented as political funding and my business rivals painted me as some sort of conspirator. Soon my telephones began to be tapped. I had no clue that these allegations were being shored up against me till a close friend who worked in the government sought me out. 'What are you doing?' he asked angrily, 'Financing General Zia's overthrow? Why are you sending money to Benazir?' I was taken aback and soon realized a political case was being built against me. I was advised by other friends to leave the country. 'The government is going to come down very hard on you,' one of them warned me. I said I would stay and fight it out. I had done nothing wrong, I would not run.

The raid began at 7 a.m. A team of forty people, dressed in civilian clothes and headed by the director of the Federal Investigation Agency (FIA), virtually occupied my house in Karachi. Rather than knock at the door or ring the bell, they climbed the wall and broke in—as if they were conquering an enemy country. Every room was ransacked, cupboards were opened, and clothes and books and papers were thrown on the floor. Pillows were cut up to see if secret papers or perhaps gold had been hidden inside. My young daughters were still in their nightdresses but were rudely brushed aside by a group of men who showed no sensitivity or courtesy for their privacy. My ageing mother was so shocked that she fainted. I was told the FIA squad was searching for 'incriminating documents' that would establish my role in the 'plot' against the government. There was no plot and there were no such documents but who was going to listen in that mad, intrigue-filled moment? It was four hours of humiliation. In exasperation, I told an assistant director of the FIA, who was part of the raid, 'You won't find anything, so plant something [some forged document] if you want to.' I will never forget his reply: 'That we don't do. I have a conscience.' He was a good man; we were all good people in Pakistan. What had our governments and politicians done to us and to our moral compass?

My brother Akbar and his family lived on the first floor of the house. It was there that the FIA team found a bottle of Tia Maria, the rum-based liqueur. The raiding party was exultant, as if it had discovered a nuclear bomb. Akbar was arrested for violating prohibition laws. I was told that there was a case of evasion of 3 lakh rupees of excise duties against Premier Tobacco and I was being charged. The case had been propped up by a rival in the tobacco business. In any case, I was more an investor than a manager in Premier Tobacco, which was run by salaried executives. Following the raid, I was taken to the Jinnah Hospital and admitted there for a few hours. A doctor came to take a blood sample from my arm. A few minutes later, he returned to ask me, '*Aap sharaab peete ho* (Do you drink alcohol)?' He spoke in Urdu but from his accent I realized he was Sindhi. So I replied in Sindhi and told him I didn't drink at all. 'You are Sindhi?' the doctor responded. 'You are my brother . . . I have been asked to implicate you in a false case and certify that traces of alcohol have been found in your blood.' He was urged to testify that I was drunk when brought to the hospital at about 1 p.m., as if I had spent the whole morning drinking, even while my house was being raided. Apparently, calls had come to the hospital from Junejo's office and from his secretary Iqbal—being from Sindh, the PM knew people in Karachi—but the good doctor refused to lie. I could not be charged with breaking the prohibition laws that applied to Muslims.

From the hospital, I was taken to the FIA's offices on Queen's Road. I was detained there for two days. My brother too had been brought in, arrested in the Tia Maria bottle case. I felt sorry for Akbar. He was being punished because he was my brother; I was the government's target, not him. In any case, the FIA had erred. Under the law, possession of alcohol was not a crime, only drinking was, if you were a Muslim. As such, Akbar's arrest was incorrect. I asked an officer to put the charge of possessing the Tia Maria bottle against my name. It would be one more charge added to the many they had made against me. Meanwhile, Akbar would be free to go home. However, the officer shook his head. 'We can't do that,' he said. 'The case has already been registered against your brother. We cannot withdraw it.' I applied for bail since all the offences I had been accused of were bailable. The judge was told by the government to reject my application, which he did. I was to be sent to regular prison. As I said to my lawyer, 'I am not being handcuffed, that is the only mercy.' Some of my friends found out about the pressure on the judge and requested him to reconsider. He did and, following a review petition, the rejection of bail was revoked. I was free to go home, arriving to be greeted by my wife and children, sister and mother. As I sat down for lunch with my mother, a senior politician rang up. Elahi Buksh Soomro was an old friend and his voice betrayed anxiety. 'Where are you? Get out of Karachi at once. They want to arrest you again . . . They are filing a case against you on MPO.' Then he hurriedly hung up. I was left speechless. MPO was an abbreviation for 'Maintenance of Public Order'. It was a legal clause invoked when a person posed a risk to society and a threat to public peace. Being arrested under MPO provisions meant that a person could spend up to ninety days in prison without being allowed to seek bail. Who knew what would happen in police custody— torture, coercion, anything was possible.

Immediately I left home, spending the night at a friend's house on the outskirts of Karachi. The next morning I flew to Islamabad, the ticket having been booked under another name. The authorities had sent a posse of policemen to my hotel in Islamabad in case I turned up there. I avoided the hotel and went to the house of a businessman friend, the late Asaf Ali. There I found out that there was a nationwide alert for me. It was as if I had been declared a traitor and an enemy of the people. This was absolutely crazy. I realized I had to reach out to someone senior in Islamabad. I went to the residence of Aslam Khattak, the interior minister. He was shocked to see me, and said, '*Tum kya kar rahe ho idhar? Tumhara humne [MPO] file sign kiya hai* (What are you doing here? I've signed your [MPO] file).' Through common friends I sent word to Junejo and General Zia, telling them what was happening to me was a gross miscarriage of justice. They refused to see me or intervene. After three days, I tried to enter my hotel but there were policemen in the lobby and I slipped away. I drove to a friend's house in Rawalpindi, Islamabad's twin city, bought new clothes and medicines that I used, and vanished into the country, driving from place to place in rural Punjab. I was at the end of my wits. Finally, I was shown a way out by Mian Habibullah, a prominent member of the Muslim League who was close to both Zia, and Junejo, as well as me. He sent me a message advising me to seek the intervention of the Pir Pagara, Syed Shah Mardan Shah II. He was the seventh Pir Pagara, who passed away in 2012 and was succeeded by his son, the eighth and current Pir. The Pir Pagara was a respected religious and social leader, one of the best-known Pakistanis. He was head of the Hurs, an order of Sufi Muslims, and his moral authority was rooted in, among other things, the fact that his father had been hanged by the British during the anti-colonial struggle. If he interceded on my behalf, Habibullah said, maybe General Zia would relent. We met at Habibullah's house in Lahore and it was the first time I had the privilege of an audience with the Pir Pagara. He came straight to the point: 'So have you given money to the girl [a reference to Benazir]?'

'No, Pir Sahib, I have not.'

'But what about these conversations of yours with Pyar Ali Allana . . .'

I explained the context to him, including the trust fund that Ghulam Ali Allana had left. 'I swear I haven't given Benazir or anybody else from her party political funding. I have never even met her. This is a conspiracy of my business rivals in the tobacco industry . . .'

The Pir Pagara nodded his head and stayed silent for a while. Then he spoke cryptically: 'Okay . . . Let me see what I can do . . .'

After a few days, I got a message that I was free to go back to Karachi. The Pir Sahib had spoken to Junejo and to General Zia. The MPO warrant had been withdrawn, though the excise and other cases would stay. The spiritual leader had saved me. I returned to Karachi and stayed for a few days before leaving for London and Los Angeles, where one of my daughters had to be taken for surgery. When she recovered, we flew back to Pakistan. The experience of being a fugitive in my own country had shaken me. It took a few months for me to get back to normal, catching up with work and trying to deal with the barrage of legal cases. At least there was no immediate threat of a midnight knock on the door and of being bundled into a police van.

There is a piquant, even funny postscript to all this. A few days after the raid on my house, Benazir spoke to Pyar Ali Allana. 'So where is the money that you got from Hashwani?' she demanded. 'Why hasn't it come to me or the party?' Even she believed the government's propaganda!

7

A STRING OF PEARLS

Even as Zia and his cronies were needling and harassing me, my business was making steady progress. I had moved into real estate development and built a few commercial and shopping plazas in Karachi besides, of course, managing two successful hotels. As a representative of Continental Grain, I was still sourcing rice from Pakistan. Since buying and selling between private players had stopped following nationalization, I had to negotiate and deal with the Rice Corporation of Pakistan, set up by the government, and buy rice as an agent of Continental. I did the paperwork on behalf of Continental and my other overseas principals, took possession of the rice and shipped it. In return, Continental and the other companies paid me a commission.

Since I was being paid in dollars and earning foreign exchange for Pakistan, I was allowed to retain some of the money abroad. I used this to pay for my travels and, more importantly, to pay for my children's education in Britain and later the US. The experience of starting two hotels had whetted my appetite, however, and this was clearly the field I wanted to do more in. An opportunity came my way in 1985, a year before the MPO episode that I described in the preceding chapter. The government decided to privatize Pakistan Services Limited (PSL), which had a portfolio of four hotels—in Karachi, Lahore, Rawalpindi and Peshawar. The four hotels had been built by the government decades earlier and had suffered greatly at the hands of bureaucrats who knew nothing of the hospitality industry. All four were managed by the InterContinental Group but, though they bore the InterContinental logo, they were anything but world-class luxury or business hotels. Rather than drain even more public money, some technocrats in the government recommended selling the company altogether and letting an appropriate private business group run the hotels. The Banking Council of Pakistan was tasked with calling for bids. I put in my bid and was shortlisted, qualifying on the basis of my experience in the hotel industry as well as my financial credentials. It would not have escaped notice that my hotel in Karachi (today, the Marriott) was beating the government-owned hotel hollow and was clearly more popular than the InterContinental.

Going over the shortlist, I realized my closest competition would come from two people. The first was Mir Afzal Khan, a wealthy and well-connected man from the North West Frontier Province (now called Khyber Pakhtunkhwa) who was leading a consortium that included professional hoteliers. Mir Afzal Khan was no pushover. In fact, in the 1990s, he went on to become chief minister of his province. The second was Mahmoud Abdullah Haroon of Dawn Group, chairman of one of Pakistan's most influential media conglomerates. Coming from an old and distinguished family, Haroon was active in public life, had served as a minister—in fact, he was a minister at the time the bids were opened—and went on to become Governor of Sindh. He was said to be supported by the Galadhari Brothers, the well-known business group based in Dubai. Haroon and the Galadharis had an old association, having collaborated to launch the *Khaleej Times* newspaper in 1978. As investors, the Galadhari Brothers already owned 17 per cent of PSL. Rather than a 51 per cent stake, Haroon and his partners would even have settled for 34 per cent— had the government negotiators insisted—as that would have given the Galadhari-backed bidder majority control of PSL. It would be a tough battle against such formidable contenders. What I was glad about was that the public officials overseeing the high-profile privatization were men of unimpeachable integrity. Ghulam Ishaq Khan, a very experienced public servant, was the finance minister. Khan, who was to succeed General Zia as Pakistan's President in 1988, could be rigid and unbending but was scrupulously honest. He played by the rules and would not change or manipulate them to suit political interests. Working under him was H.U. Baig, the finance secretary, also an upright and competent civil servant, one of the best in Pakistan.

When the bids were examined, it came down to a battle between the three big aspirants. The chairman of the Banking Council of Pakistan called all of us to lunch in Karachi to settle terms and discuss options as we approached the ultimate decision. Till then, I had kept my cards close to my chest and decided on my strategy ahead of the lunch meeting, which I knew would be crucial. Competitive negotiations of this nature are a game of poker. Your key weapon is phlegmatic secrecy—not letting your opponents know where you really stand. If you can fool them into believing you are weaker than you are, all the better. It goes without saying that this has to be done with utmost subtlety. All along I had projected that I was not a serious bidder, and would be willing to step down if cajoled or paid off by one of the other bidders. This was a bluff. To strengthen the perception, one of my companies went to the Dubai Bank, owned by Galadhari Brothers, and requested a small overdraft. The news spread throughout the business community and many began to believe I had cash flow problems. This was exactly the picture I had set out to convey. After lunch on that fateful day in Karachi, each bidder was called in for a one-to-one meeting with the Banking Council team handling the privatization process. I was called in first but said I would defer to the status of my seniors and go after them. Mir Afzal Khan was the first to go into the meeting room. He came out in fifteen minutes, looking confused. 'Should I congratulate you?' I asked. 'No,' he said, pulling a face, 'it's too complicated.' Khawaja Abdur Rehman, representing the Dawn Group, went in next. He spent almost an hour in the meeting room. When he came out, his face was red with anger. One glance at him and I knew that he had fought a pitched battle inside and that there had been contentious arguments. He stomped off without saying a word.

It was my turn. As I sat down, I was told the price I'd bid—all bids were presented to the Banking Council in sealed envelopes—was too low and couldn't be accepted. I showed no emotion and said calmly that the reputation of the Karachi hotel was such that it had 'more cockroaches than guests'. 'It could be the pride of Pakistan,' I added, 'but has been driven to the ground . . . The operator, InterContinental, is making money by way of a management fee, but not the owner . . . Don't you want to restore the image of Pakistan?' The negotiators changed the subject. 'We want more than what you have bid,' I was told. I looked hard and straight at the chairman, the chief negotiator, and asked, 'I have a blunt question, please don't get offended. Does the committee have the authority to sell the hotels or only to bargain?' 'What do you mean?' The chairman was livid. 'Go outside please,' he said, 'we will call you.' I walked out without batting an eyelid.

My inference was that the negotiating team was too nervous, trying too hard. One bidder had walked out calling the auction 'too complicated', the other had departed in anger. I was the only one left. This was a critical mandate and the Banking Council members would have wanted to make a success of it. Even though they were talking tough with me, I could tell they were anxious. I was playing a better game of poker than them. After thirty minutes, they called me back to the meeting room and said that they had telephoned the finance ministry in Islamabad for instructions. Ghulam Ishaq Khan had confirmed that the Banking Council team had the authority to conclude the deal and actually finalize the sale of PSL. 'Excellent,' I said, 'so let's agree to a price and finish it.' We bargained and reached a figure that was higher than my initial bid, closer to what the Council wanted. I was asked to bring in 50 lakh rupees as an additional deposit, to increase the deposit I would pay when submitting the bid documents. 'I'll do that right away,' I said, 'but I want the acceptance letter at once.' They nodded and I rushed to my office, a short walk away. I took out my Bank of America chequebook, wrote out and signed a cheque, and was back at the Banking Council within a few minutes. Handing over the cheque, I asked for the acceptance letter. 'Come back tomorrow, we'll have it ready,' I was told. 'No sir, not tomorrow,' I was polite but firm, 'I want it today. That was our agreement.' 'Fair enough,' said the chairman, 'give us an hour.' An hour later, I had a letter confirming the success of my bid and naming me the new owner of PSL, provided I met the residual payment obligations. I went back to my office with a smirk, but knew that a second battle would start in a few hours.

I was proved right. The next morning, there was much consternation in Karachi and Islamabad. The Dawn Group went to court but the judge refuse to strike down the transaction or intervene otherwise. I was not a favourite of General Zia's anyway and Haroon was then a minister in the federal government. He rushed to the general, complaining and demanding that Zia step in to deny me the hotels. Zia himself was quite angry and summoned Ghulam Ishaq Khan. The finance minister stood his ground and defended what he called a transparent deal, making it plain that he couldn't negate the agreement simply because someone didn't like Sadruddin Hashwani's face! The general said no more, knowing it was futile to ask Ghulam Ishaq Khan to compromise and that he was constrained by a bewildering and unlikely system of checks and balances that can thwart even military dictators in Pakistan. Zia then called Baig and asked him to travel to Karachi without informing Ghulam Ishaq Khan and scrutinize the circumstances of the transaction. Baig went to the Banking Council office and took possession of all relevant documents, bringing them back to Islamabad to study. A few days later, he submitted his report, saying the deal was completely above board. This was conveyed to Zia. I was asked to pay the rest of the money and the shares of PSL were transferred to me. From two hotels, I now came to control six, including two in my native city, Karachi. A new chapter had begun in my life.

Having gained possession of the hotels, it was now my chance to prove I could restore them to their former glory. InterContinental had the management contract for all four hotels. Each time the contract expired, they made sure they got a renewal on generous terms, using the US embassy and political friends to twist the arm of the Pakistan government. When I took charge of PSL, InterContinental approached me to seek a renewal of the management contract. I played hardball. 'No,' I told InterContinental's local representative, 'no management contract. I want a franchise. Like I have a Holiday Inn franchise for my other hotels . . .' Taken aback, he wrote to his superiors for instructions. A few days later, the regional (Asia-Pacific) managing director for InterContinental, Ken Roofe, flew in from Honolulu. Our meeting was short and curt—I insisted on a franchise or there would be no deal. 'I'm sorry, we won't give you the franchise,' Roofe said. 'We don't give franchises.' He was being less than truthful. 'You have given the InterContinental franchise to the Taj Group in Bombay,' I reminded him. 'My Holiday Inn hotels are run better and do better than your InterContinental hotels in Pakistan. It is because my hotels gave you such competition and put a dent in your operations that PSL suffered losses and the government was forced to sell. And now you tell me that I'm not competent enough to get your franchise?' Roofe had no real answer. He said he'd consult his headquarters in New York. The board met in New York to consider the matter and decided it was contract renewal or nothing. 'If you don't renew our management contract,' Roofe told me two days later, 'we will take away our flag in thirty days.' They were trying to break me, confident I didn't have the gumption to start afresh at four hotels in thirty days. In response, I invited Roofe home for dinner.

By then, I had moved to a new house on Clifton's Bath Island. I had begun living there in 1976 and started to build the house of my dreams. I had even bought imported sanitaryware from the market. I later discovered that it had been sourced from other hotel project promoters who had brought in surplus equipment, misusing the import licence given to them to furbish their hotels. It surprised many people that I had not done the same thing—simply pilfering and diverting sanitaryware imported for my hotels in Karachi and Islamabad for my private use, especially since I was finalizing plans for my own house at the same time. It was at this house—which we sold in early 2014—that Roofe and his colleagues arrived. I served the InterContinental delegation a grand dinner—succulent lobsters, the choicest seafood, the works. As he was leaving, Roofe asked, 'I haven't got an answer from you. No response to our board's decision?' 'Oh that,' I said, smiling my biggest smile, 'actually, I wanted you to enjoy the food. Okay, in thirty days I'll give your flag back to you . . . Goodnight!' His jaw dropped. This was the last thing he had expected. What he didn't know was that I had already begun going through the inventory. It was not just the flag. In thirty days, a total of 468 items had to be changed—including the logo in front of the hotels, the cutlery with 'InterContinental' embossed on forks and knives and spoons, the crockery with its monogram, the letterhead, the names on all the stationery . . . The drill started the very next morning.

First, we paid whatever we still owed InterContinental. Then I sought suggestions for a name for the new chain of hotels. I had decided on a name anyway—Pearl Continental Hotels—but asked consultants and advertising agencies all the same. It seemed like the professional thing to do. We began to place orders for all the items the hotels would need. Since there was a shortage of skilled Pakistani hotel professionals in those days—hotel management schools and courses were not as popular as they are now—I sought out well-regarded names from other countries for general managerial positions. On the thirtieth day, we ceremoniously lowered the InterContinental flag and unfurled the new flag. It was a big event at each of the hotels, a goodbye and also the celebration of a new arrival. Pearl Continental—or PC, as regular users of our hotels were to affectionately call it—was on its way.

Not having to pay a fat management contract fee to InterContinental was a blessing as it saved us a considerable sum. As we rationalized hotel expenses, the money helped us improve the balance sheet and spare resources to upgrade our properties. We started rebuilding what were potentially very good hotels but had gone to seed. I hired new people and treated the entrenched worker unions at each of the hotels with tact. I wanted the old employees to see the new owners as partners and friends but also as professional managers, demanding efficiency and quality.

It was important to bring discipline and courtesy to what were essentially customer-driven businesses and geared towards guest satisfaction. To win the trust of employees, I started various training programmes for hotel staff members so that they too felt they were learning with the company.

Gradually, we began to make profits. With 300 rooms, the Karachi hotel was the largest of the ones we had bought. The hotels in Lahore and Rawalpindi had 200 rooms each and the Pearl Continental Peshawar began with 150 rooms. All of these have expanded significantly. Take Pearl Continental Lahore—we built a new wing, the Atrium Wing, and trebled capacity by adding 400 rooms. It bloomed like Cinderella and came to be recognized as a genuine five-star hotel, lavish and luxurious. I don't like choosing between my hotels but, if you ask me, I honestly think the Pearl Continental Lahore is the best hotel in Pakistan. Meanwhile, in the mid-1980s, shortly after the PSL acquisition, I began to build a second wing in the Islamabad hotel (now the Marriott) and complete it to its planned 300-room capacity. At my original hotel in Karachi (also the Marriott now), I began constructing a series of banquet halls as well as a 600-car underground parking below Bagh-e-Jinnah, which you will recall was near the hotel.

Both the Marriotts and all four Pearl Continental hotels (close to a dozen today) became popular fairly quickly.

The discotheque at the Karachi Marriott was the life of the city, drawing throngs of young people every evening. One evening in 1983, I remember it was a Thursday, I got a call at home at 11.30 p.m. from Christian G. Windfer, the GM. 'There's chaos in the disco!' he said. 'We've had a fight between two men and their groups . . . guns and firing. The place is full . . . There are lots of young women running about in panic. It's chaotic.' I was puzzled that he was even calling me to ask what to do. Surely he knew? 'Windfer,' I said in a deliberate tone, 'you are the GM. You have a posse of bouncers. You have black belts [in karate] at your service. Grab those fellows and throw them out. Kick them on their backsides if you need to.' With that I put down the telephone, confident that Windfer would follow my directions to the letter. He did. I thought nothing of the matter and went to sleep.

The next morning, I was awakened by a call from Haakim Ali Zardari, a minor Sindhi feudal and political wheeler-dealer with whom I had a nodding acquaintance. 'What have you done?' he thundered. 'Where did you get the courage to do what you did to my son?' It seemed the two hotheads who had begun the argument that turned into a gunfight the previous evening in the disco were Asif Ali Zardari, Haakim Ali's playboy son, and a young man from the Zehri family, which headed a prominent Baloch tribe. Windfer had duly thrown them both out;

the bouncers had delivered a few blows as well. I wasn't going to let him or his team down. 'If this is your son's character,' I told Haakim Ali Zardari, 'why don't you keep him at home? Don't send him to hotels with guns to disturb civilized society. In my hotel, we don't misbehave with good people. I shake hands even with the sweeper.'

The telephone call ended acrimoniously. I shrugged my shoulders and continued with my day. Four years later, of all the men in the world and in Karachi, Benazir chose Asif Ali Zardari to marry. As I found out then, he hadn't forgotten how he was thrown out and banned from my hotel that evening in 1983. He still holds a grudge—but that's a story to be told later.

8

A ROOM WITH A VIEW

While my hotel chain was being built slowly, link by link, my personal life was going through storms and tragedies. My brother Hasan Ali's death in 1974 was a shock from which I have perhaps still not recovered. You can accept the passing of a grandparent or an ageing uncle but to lose your dear brother at the age of forty-two is a misfortune I would not wish upon anyone. Three years later, my father also left us. He had been ailing for some time and had been taken to London for the removal of his thyroid gland, which had turned malignant. He never did recover completely. It was 8.30 a.m. on 14 May 1977. I was in my room when my son Murtaza, then only three, knocked and said that his grandfather wasn't well. Seated on a chair, he had slipped into a coma. Even before a doctor arrived, he waved his hand, shed a final tear from his right eye, and was gone. A quiet, unassuming man, he died the way he lived—without troubling anybody, without making a fuss. When my brother Akbar and I picked him up, he felt as light as a baby. It was as if the burdens of the world had been taken from him. My father's death, coming so soon after Hasan Ali's, made me feel much older than my years. They also made me more aware of my duties as a father and the importance of educating my children.

In 1981, I sent my two older daughters, Nadia and Shazia, to the Jesus and Mary Convent in Murree, a hill station near Islamabad. Founded in the early nineteenth century, it is one of the best boarding schools for girls in Pakistan. Every fortnight, I used to visit my daughters, flying to Islamabad and then driving up to Murree. One day, I took them for a picnic to Bhurban, a small, picturesque town about 10 km from Murree. At 7000 feet above sea level, Bhurban was higher than Murree (6000 feet) and made for a spectacular vantage point. Nestled in the Himalayas, it offered a great view of the mountains and of the Kashmir Valley. The nearby forests were verdant. Bhurban had a nine-hole golf course on which my daughters and I walked, before settling down to a lunch of sandwiches I'd brought along from the hotel in Islamabad. At that moment, I had an epiphany. I decided to build a hotel in Bhurban.

The town was still unspoilt and sparsely populated. Land was available at a throwaway price: 5000 rupees a canal (600 yards). However, I requested the Punjab government to lease a piece of forest land—which I couldn't buy because it was government property—for a hotel. I began planning a boutique, fifty-room hotel. But it seemed too ambitious. There was no supply of cooking gas or electricity. Locals used to collect water for domestic use from natural streams. The design that emerged from the fifty-room mandate given to the architects was not sufficient to justify or evoke the beauty of the mountains. The proposal was thus expanded to 100 rooms. We began excavating the mountainside and moving building material on donkeys. This was in the late 1980s, the same time during which we had begun the expansion of the Pearl Continental Lahore. Today, the Pearl Continental Bhurban has six floors. It just grew and grew as we worked. From the upper storeys, there is an ethereal two-sided view of the mountains. It is difficult to imagine what we went through to build the hotel. The conditions were rough and the winter was harsh, with cold winds sweeping in. It was hard for workers to access the site and to move material from Karachi right to the heart of Pakistan and then up the mountains. That aside, each time I went up to Bhurban, I changed the plans—and my changes had to be accommodated without damaging the architectural integrity of the hotel blueprint. On one visit, it struck me that we could consider building a convention hotel. So it came to be. Half the hotel was built when we decided to add a banquet hall, a squash court, meeting rooms, additional kitchens for the convention area and a 1000-person amphitheatre that most people thought would be impossible to achieve. We even constructed a helipad. Since it was in a seismic zone, the building was designed to absorb severe shocks. Enhancing electricity capacity for its operations through fuel generators, the hotel came to be centrally air-conditioned or heated—as the weather demanded—from the very first day.

The Pearl Continental Bhurban was opened in 1992 and inaugurated by Mian Muhammad Nawaz Sharif, then in his first term as PM. At the opening ceremony, I spoke of how I had visited Bhurban with my daughters and of my dream of a hotel project that would not just bring in tourists but also benefit local people and revitalize the local economy. 'Frankly, God knew,' I said, 'and in my heart I knew what would happen to this valley. I wanted the benefit to go to the people who had lived here for centuries, not to outsiders.' As the project neared completion, Bhurban's potential as a tourist and convention destination became apparent to others. The ancillary businesses that would be triggered by the hotel, providing jobs to locals, also became clear. Others too planned smaller hotels and land prices began to shoot up. When the hotel opened formally, neighbouring land was available for 90,000 rupees for a canal. It had increased eighteen-fold in a decade. Today, it is valued at much, much more. Yet, through the construction period, I refused to buy land in Bhurban and refused to allow those associated with the project—colleagues and contractors—to buy land either. I did not want crude profiteering. I wanted local residents to gain.

One person who lived near the hotel and worked for us as a driver during construction finally sold his ancestral land for a fortune. He used the money to buy a Toyota Corolla that he rented out; to build a house for his family; and to educate his children at Lahore University. Gradually, Bhurban became a destination to be reckoned with and numerous independent restaurants and hotels came up. The hotel incubated a tourism boom and put Bhurban on the map. I saw it not just as a business risk that paid off but as the legacy of a socially responsible enterprise. I was deliriously happy. The day after the formal inauguration, the hotel opened for business and we celebrated with a concert by the late Nusrat Fateh Ali Khan, Pakistan's best-known vocalist. The chief guest was a close friend, General Asif Nawaz Janjua, then the Chief of Army Staff and one of the most professional generals in the volatile history of the Pakistan military.

Later, my association with General Asif Nawaz discomfited others and led to some people attempting to poison Nawaz Sharif's ears. In truth, there was nothing even remotely political about the friendship—we just got along as individuals. Nevertheless, in a Pakistan teeming with conspiracy theories and given the troubled history of relations between the army and civilian governments, all sorts of rumours were spread. To add to it, the expansion of Pearl Continental Lahore was delayed because construction took longer than expected. This upset Nawaz Sharif, who was keen that his home city got a first-rate hotel as soon as possible. Perhaps he thought I was deliberately delaying things, which was not true as I too was worried about my capital being blocked. Finally, the new wing of the Lahore hotel opened in 1997. Shahbaz Sharif, Nawaz Sharif's brother, was then the chief minister of Punjab and inaugurated the hotel. Close to two decades have passed since; it is ironical that Nawaz Sharif is back as PM of Pakistan, a mature, seasoned politician, now into his third term, and that Shahbaz Sharif is back as a very successful chief minister of Punjab.

Just like the hotel project in Bhurban, my next big hotel start-up—in Muzaffarabad, the capital of Azad Jammu and Kashmir—was also a shot in the dark. This hotel was and remains a bet on the future and cannot be explained in terms of immediate revenues or financial gains. It has a backstory that necessitates retelling. In 1947, the kingdom of Jammu and Kashmir had a majority Muslim population but a Hindu king. Disaffection broke out in the Kashmir region, an idyllic and beauteous area soon becoming a conflict zone. War broke out between Pakistan and India. Kashmir came to be divided between Azad Jammu and Kashmir, which is under Pakistani protection, and the Kashmir Valley, which has faced the onslaught of Indian guns and jackboots for almost seventy years. I am not a historian or a politician and I don't know where the solution to the Kashmir problem lies. What I do know is that a solution has to be found that is fair to the unfortunate people of Kashmir and respects the dignity of both Pakistan and India. Whichever way I look at it, trade has to be a component of this solution. Kashmir lies at the intersection of ancient trade routes. In the past, the Silk Road passed through it, connecting Central and South Asia. Can we expect a future where caravans of goods and travellers will journey from Srinagar to Muzaffarabad to the Karakoram Highway and into western China?

This was the question I asked myself in 2002, when I flew to Muzaffarabad to recce the site. The government of Azad Jammu and Kashmir was reluctant to give me the site that I had shortlisted. It had been reserved for construction of the official residence of the President of Azad Jammu and Kashmir. Located on a hill, it offered a panoramic view of the Neelam Valley and the Jhelum River. One look at it and I felt there was no prettier place on earth. It took all my persuasive skills to get the local government to agree to let me build my hotel at this location. In October 2005, two years after we began construction, there was an earthquake in Kashmir and across northern Pakistan. Tens of thousands of people died and villages on the outskirts of Muzaffarabad were razed to the ground. We had to stop construction and re-examine the structure. Our plans had accounted for an earthquake of magnitude 7 on the Richter scale. The 2005 earthquake was much more powerful. I insisted that we reinforce the structure and make it strong enough to sustain an earthquake of magnitude 10. This was unnecessary, I was told—an earthquake of that magnitude had never occurred in known human history. I wasn't listening. Of course, the reinforcement was expensive and the budget went up by close to 40 per cent. Never mind. It allowed me to sleep peacefully at night—and has allowed the hotel guests to sleep peacefully as well.

A section of the hotel opened in 2007 and it went into full operation in 2011. In 2002, when I had conceived of the hotel, there was practically zero trade between the parts of Kashmir administered by Pakistan and by India. People—some of them Kashmiris from the same family or clan—were not allowed to travel from one part of Kashmir to the other. Muzaffarabad was a small, hilly, agricultural own, scarcely a bustling business or tourist city. Next door, in Afghanistan, war raged. Yet, I was convinced that the urgings for peace would overcome all else; that politicians in both India and Pakistan would look for answers in negotiations and not bullets; and that people from both parts of Kashmir, and both countries, would travel, trade with and greet each other as friends. I felt that the world situation and the changing instincts of politicians in both New Delhi and Islamabad would create conditions for commerce and tourism in the composite Kashmir region. This was not to be.

I keep visiting my 102-room hotel. It is calm and serene as ever. It is at peace with nature. Like me, it is waiting for humans to make peace with themselves.

My hotels are more than just businesses for me. To be frank, I have indulged myself and my fantasies with some of my hotel projects and taken decisions that strict commercial considerations would not recommend. Business is not merely about playing safe. One of my principal disagreements with the big American or European investment banks is that once they put in money and buy equity in a company, they force the company's management to live from quarter to quarter, tailoring the work process to suit the stock market's expectations. Admittedly, this does usher in discipline but it also curtails ambitions and inspired risks. A businessman who is free of the tyranny of Wall Street's calculators can potentially do things differently. He can think like a genuine entrepreneur.

Once in a while, he will be wrong and his plans will fail but when he succeeds, the success will be so spectacular that it will take one's breath away.

I have experienced such heady emotions with some of my hotel projects, particularly Bhurban, which I am extremely proud of as it was only an idea in my head when we started out. Some years ago, Tariq Aziz—who is a college friend of Pervez Musharraf's and served as secretary in the National Security Council when Musharraf was President—sent me a very moving letter. Aziz's elderly, ailing father wanted a change of scenery and his son took him to the Pearl Continental Bhurban. Aziz's father— who passed away shortly afterwards, unfortunately—was enthralled by the majestic beauty of the location. Seated on the balcony one evening, he told his son, 'Whoever had a vision to build this will surely go to paradise.' When I read those words, my eyes welled up. The senior gentleman's blessings warmed my soul. More than cheques and dividends, profits and windfalls, these are the moments one cherishes as a businessman.

Strangely, I have not ended up staying much in my hotels. When friends ask me why, I shrug my shoulders and say, 'My quest is elsewhere.' In twenty years, I have slept only nine nights at the Bhurban hotel. I stayed there during the opening, attending the Nusrat Fateh Ali Khan concert, and on two occasions later, both of which coincided with musical events—concerts by Farida Khanum and Iqbal Bano. I attended the Farida Khanum concert quite unexpectedly. A friend from London was visiting me in Islamabad. He was depressed because his business was facing problems. To cheer him up, I drove him to Bhurban, to experience the magic of the hotel and the mountains and to listen to Farida. His depression left him, at least during the time he was in Bhurban. To have been able to give my friend a few hours of happiness was worth its weight in gold. Those sharp suits on Wall Street will never understand such sentiments.

While we were living in Karachi, the Marriott became a venue for some of my close friends to gather for a private evening every fortnight. Five or six couples would get together and ask a ghazal singer to come and sing for us in a room requisitioned for the occasion. We pooled to pay the artiste's fee. It became our ritual. One evening in February 1983, I was playing squash at Karachi Gymkhana, close to the Marriott, when I heard a loud sound. I didn't know it then but there had been a rocket attack on the Holiday Inn (as the hotel was then called). The target was the Air France office on the ground floor. Unaware of this, I continued playing. A few minutes later, my brother came banging down the door of the squash court, panicking and panting. He told me of the attack. I asked for ten minutes to finish the game, to allow me to gather my thoughts, and then left for the Marriott. What I saw can only be described in one word: chaos. Thankfully, nobody had died and the fire brigade had arrived but the confusion seemed unending. I took charge and got everybody from the GM to the janitor involved in cleaning up the site and removing burnt material. The injured were rushed to hospital. In three hours, we had repaired things to the extent required and the hotel was back in commission. That was when I got a call from a friend. 'Sadru,' he began, 'I heard about the attack. Is the ghazal party off?' 'No, it's on,' I said. 'See you in an hour. I just need to go home and wash up.' Our hotel was not really the target. A militant group wanted to attack Air France to send a signal to the French government, as part of the politics being played out during the Iran–Iraq war. What I hadn't realized as I left the hotel for home was that there had been several attacks on French targets, including diplomats, in the city. The fates had sent me a warning. I had set out to build my hotels as oases of calm and hospitality. As it happened, evil was never far away. This was the first terror attack on any of my hotels. The deadliest, of course, was a quarter-century away.

~

My hotel business also took me overseas. In 1989, I was approached by a group of Ismaili businessmen to invest in hotel projects in Canada and the US. I agreed, encouraged by the fact that Tota and Lisbona had also offered to invest with me. Unfortunately, the key person in the arrangement, a pious but crooked man living in London, cheated me. I couldn't comprehend how someone who claimed to have deep faith in God could also have the instincts of a petty thief, but this man was just such a person. A quarter-century has passed but I am still struggling to recover my money. Nevertheless, I began to invest in hotels in the US as part of a consortium. I was very keen on a property in Houston as I was getting interested in the oil and gas business. Houston was and still is the energy capital of Texas and of the US. I hired a consultant to identify a suitable hotel in Houston and we began to consider the Sheraton downtown. It was being foreclosed by Citibank. We did our homework and started negotiating, eventually landing in Houston to sign the agreement. We met the Citibank executives and the meeting went well. The next morning, I walked into the hotel that I was about to purchase. To my surprise, I saw a marketplace. A huge crowd was milling about as fixtures and fittings and TVs and furniture were being auctioned off. The hotel owed some taxes to the civic authorities and instead of paying, or even mentioning it to me, some clever mind in Citibank had decided to ransack and virtually denude the hotel to raise money for the taxes. Items collectively worth millions were being sold for next to nothing. I was very angry. Citibank had acted in bad faith and there was no point taking over the shell of a hotel. I walked out on the deal and to pacify myself went for a walk down the streets of Houston. Having calmed myself, I went to the coffee shop of the Hyatt Regency, where I was staying, and had coffee with my consultant. We talked of the disappointment of the deal having gone sour. As we left the table, I exclaimed, 'One day, God will give us a hotel in Houston . . . Perhaps this hotel . . .' Those final words were uttered with a smile, with me waving my hands and pointing to our surroundings and the hotel we were in.

That evening I was free. I was booked to fly to London and then to Pakistan the following day. To keep myself busy, I decided to do a tour of the Hyatt Regency, a 1000-room convention hotel. This was not unusual for me. When I stay in a hotel for the first time, I try to get to know it better. In part, this is plain inquisitiveness. In part, it is a desire to learn more about the hotel industry, for it engrosses me. That evening, I strolled up and down the Hyatt, seeing the housekeeping staff at work in empty rooms, encountering the kitchen crew, chatting up front desk executives. I could tell the hotel was a bit run-down but had potential. With those stray thoughts, I went back to my room, packed my bags and slept, having set the alarm for the morning and for the drive to the airport.

This book is a tribute to my forefathers, my role models who left the greatest of human legacies for their successor generations: faith, truth and honesty. May their blessings always keep us on the right path.

Great-grandfather
Mukhi Hashoo Tharuani

Grandfather
Kamadia Abdullah Hashoo

Father, Mukhi Hussain Hashwani

Mother, Zaver Hussain Hashwani

Passionate about cricket, Sadruddin Hashwani was known for his
fast-bowling exploits in the 1950s.

Hashwani cut his teeth as a hands-on businessman touring across
Pakistan. This is the Bolan Mail, which took him from
Karachi to Quetta every two weeks.

Hashwani shared a strong, intimate bond with his mother, Zaver.

The Zaver Pearl Continental Hotel, built in the loving memory of his mother, in Gwadar, Balochistan, where she was born.

The Holiday Inn, Islamabad, built on the request of the Pakistani government, started operations in 1978.

Mr Karl Kilburg of Marriott International Inc. and Sadruddin Hashwani at the signing of the Marriott franchise, 1992.

The expanded Holiday Inn Hotel, now the Marriott, Islamabad.

Sadruddin Hashwani took the big-business community
in Pakistan by surprise when he bought the run-down but
coveted InterContinental hotels, in 1985.

He conceived of a new brand of hotels, the Pearl Continental, which is
today the leading name in luxury and hospitality in Pakistan.
(Above) Pearl Continental, Karachi, converted from
InterContinental (top).

On 20 September 2008, the Islamabad Marriott Hotel became the target of a high-intensity bomb attack, which left sixty dead and nearly 300 people injured.

Hashwani addressing a ceremony held in October 2014 to commemorate the victims of the blast.

The residence of Mukhi Hashoo since 1894 was converted into the Hashoo Museum by Sadruddin Hashwani, and was inaugurated on 11 May 2008. It houses a 400-year-old handwritten Quran, among other artefacts of historical and religious importance.

Sadruddin Hashwani addressing the first alumni meet of the Hashoo Foundation, a dynamic non-profit organization working in the areas of poverty alleviation and human development since 1988.

Hashwani with the late General Asif Nawaz Janjua, a very close friend and a thorough professional who later became Chief of the Pakistan Army.

HE Ambassador Peter Claes presents the jewel and diploma of Knight-Commander in the Order of Leopold II to Sadruddin Hashwani on behalf of HH King Philippe of Belgium, on 29 April 2014.

A few days later, the consultant telephoned me in Karachi. 'Remember the Hyatt Regency where you stayed?' he said. 'Well, there may be an opportunity to bid for it.' I felt a tingling sensation. An off-the-cuff remark had proved prophetic! The consultant then explained the circumstances. The hotel was owned by an entity that was a JV between Tenneco Oil and Prudential Insurance. Hyatt managed the hotel but was unhappy with the state of the property and had submitted a plan to refurbish it. Tenneco and Prudential had baulked at the budget of 37 million dollars. The hotel was not making money and the owners did not want to invest further without being certain of returns. I realized this was a vicious circle. Tenneco and Prudential would not put in money till the hotel began to register large profits, and the hotel would not register large profits without an overhaul. I told the consultant I was keen and, in fact, ready with an offer to 'buy the hotel as it is'. The consultant was surprised. 'But surely you want your people to do due diligence.' I didn't. 'I've done my due diligence,' I told him. In the days to come, I repeated the line to colleagues at office and friends and family members, all of whom thought I was foolhardy in buying a hotel in faraway Houston without giving it a closer look. Actually, that final evening at the Hyatt Regency had been spent very fruitfully and had given me a very good idea of the strengths and weaknesses of the hotel. That was my 'due diligence'.

In the following days, a formal bid document was prepared and sent. Tenneco and Prudential laughed at the 'unconditional offer', minus due diligence. This was unheard of in the US and they must have thought I was a rich but stupid man. The owners demanded 42 million dollars. We agreed at 40 million dollars and the deal was done. The ones most baffled were the executives from Hyatt, who managed the hotel. They now had to contend with a new owner, and one who seemed to take quick, even impulsive decisions. I assured them I intended to make a success of the hotel but felt the 37-million-dollar estimate for refurbishment was too high. In 1989 itself, I moved to Houston for three months and personally supervised the revamp of the hotel, sticking to Hyatt's specifications and demands but negotiating with contractors and sub-contractors and cutting costs without compromising quality. The hotel underwent a complete makeover that cost only 17 million dollars yet satisfied Hyatt. This became my flagship property in the US.

That first hotel deal in Houston got me thinking. Was there a business model here? Could I pick up foreclosed or under-the-weather properties and turn them around, and then run or sell them? I repeated the process with the Hilton Southwest, also in Houston. Then we bought a hotel in Boca Raton, Florida. Having revived these hotels and made them flourish, I sold them. It was difficult to manage hotels in the US while living in Pakistan. My last hotel deal in the US was in Orlando, Florida. Here too we bought a bedraggled hotel, tended to it lovingly, and sold it when it started to do well. There was a time in the 1990s when I spent sustained periods in the US, particularly in Houston, where my son Hasan Ali studied. Sarah, my youngest daughter, also went to college in Texas so our house in Houston was a buzz of activity and we still have happy memories of it.

The house had an illustrious association. One of the previous owners was John Connally, Governor of Texas in the 1960s and famous for being in the same car as President John F. Kennedy in Dallas on 22 November 1963. That day, gunshots killed President Kennedy but only wounded Governor Connally. This was my brief brush with American history. That house and those hotels are now in the past. When my children graduated and left Texas and the US, I sold my interest in the hotels and moved on. In the years after that, my hotel ventures have almost entirely been in Pakistan, with two exceptions. One of my companies has signed a JV with the Libyan Investment Fund to develop a large property complex in Tripoli, right by the Mediterranean Sea. This will include a hotel, office blocks, service apartments and a shopping arcade. This project is under construction. When the hotel is ready, we will hand over management to a reputable international chain. Much against my instincts,

I will have to sign a management contract; to run a hotel in Tripoli, with the human resource and logistical needs, will prove difficult for me. There is also a large tract of land that we have in Khartoum where we have been planning a hotel for years. Political disturbances and economic sanctions against Sudan have made the project unviable and access to bank credit very tough. Also, with the breakaway of oil-rich South Sudan in 2011, Khartoum has lost its salience to business and we will have to redraw plans for the hotel as and when we are ready to build it.

~

My significant hotel projects in the past decade have all been in Pakistan—and all of them have been driven by the hope that the next twenty years will be very different for our country and our region than the last twenty years. I have related the story of the hotel in Muzaffarabad but the more audacious project, even if I say so myself, is the hotel in Gwadar. It was built at President Musharraf's behest in 2003. He told me that Gwadar port was nearing completion but there was no first-rate hotel close by, just a small one with six rooms. He requested me to fill the gap, and to do it for Pakistan.

Gwadar is a town in Balochistan that was, as I wrote earlier, dear to me as the birthplace of my beloved mother. It offers access to the Arabian Sea and it has long been a dream of Pakistanis to see it as a thriving trading city. Gwadar was originally a part of the Sultanate of Oman. Ayub Khan's government bought it from the authorities in Muscat in 1958 because Oman, lacking oil, was short of cash. There was nothing to Gwadar except an old fort—where an earlier Sultan of Oman had once fought a battle—and a peerless sea-facing location. Could this become a second Karachi and Pakistan's major deep-sea port and trading hub? That tantalizing prospect has been contemplated by generations of Pakistanis since 1958. In 2002, the government asked a Chinese company to construct a port there. The following year, Musharraf requested me to build a hotel. This context is important because many of my Indian friends, obsessed with theoretical war games, feel that the Gwadar port is a Chinese conspiracy and naval facility. They don't realize that the desire to have a trading hub in Gwadar is a long-cherished Pakistani dream. It has nothing to do with military ambitions or global politics. It is born of a genuine belief that a major port in Gwadar can lead to exponential benefits for Pakistan's people and its economy.

When Gwadar port finally opened in 2007, its management was handed over to Singapore Port Authority. Dubai Ports World and a Chinese company were also interested in bidding for management rights, but the then Pakistani government decided to go for a Singaporean operating company. This was a strategic mistake as the Singaporeans were not up to the task and did not understand the wider implications of the port project. Gwadar can only be viable with a direct roadway to Punjab, the heartland of Pakistan. This will make it crucial to Central Asian and Afghan commerce with and through Pakistan, giving landlocked countries an opening to the sea. It can provide an alternative route from west China to West Asia. Now the Chinese have taken charge of Gwadar port from the Singaporeans and a Chinese company is constructing the highway from Gwadar to Multan. Our hotel, inaugurated in 2006, is waiting for Gwadar to boom and for the merchant ships of the world to come calling.

Pearl Continental Gwadar has been praised as an iconic hotel. It is built on a cliff of Koh-e-Batil, an imposing hill—an extinct volcano, actually—near the city's naval colony. Each one of its 114 rooms offers a view of the sea and there is ample space for expansion. While building it, we had to send labour and raw material from Karachi. We had to make housing arrangements for workers. We were building a hotel in a desolate area, with very little infrastructure. Some of my executives and contractors apprehended lawlessness but were pleasantly surprised by Balochi hospitality. Neglected by every single government in Pakistan, with poor social and economic indices, and with their resources, primarily gas, being taken away to the rest of Pakistan, Balochis are angry, and rightfully so. While building the hotel, I realized that many locals were in two minds about the construction of the port and wondered if it would make their lives better or only help outsiders. It was a legitimate question. The hotel was completed quicker than I thought but, for the moment, is near empty and losing money. For the inaugural events in 2006, I had to fly down staff and food material from my hotels in Karachi. Resources are very constrained in Gwadar. At the opening, I gave an impassioned speech in English and then switched to Balochi, much to the delight of the locals. Musharraf, who doesn't know Balochi, was unsure of what was going on and whether I was criticizing his government. He turned to Jam Mir Mohammad Yusuf, then the chief minister of Balochistan, and asked, 'What is Hashwani saying?' A year later, Musharraf came again and stayed at our hotel. This time, he was in Gwadar to inaugurate the port.

In 2013, we began work on three new hotel projects in Pakistan. The first is the Pearl Continental in Hayatabad, a modern suburb of Peshawar. We already have a Pearl Continental in the city's cantonment area. Hayatabad is a newer neighbourhood, the hub for social gatherings and business events. Peshawar, as the capital of Khyber

Pakhtunkhwa and the gateway to Afghanistan, foresees a surge in its economic importance after 2014, once the Americans leave. The second hotel is in Mirpur, where the Government of Azad Jammu and Kashmir has allowed us to build a resort—150 rooms in the first phase—overlooking a lake, with plush amenities including a theme park. Mirpur is only an hour's drive from Islamabad and I am optimistic this hotel will appeal to leisure tourists from Pakistan's capital. Finally, there is the ambitious Pearl City in Multan. We are building not just a hotel here but also 375 bungalows, shopping malls and office blocks. In all three cases, like in my earlier hotel projects, the design is being conceptualized to blend with the architecture and ethos of the host city. By end 2015, all these hotels will be ready and we would have a dozen properties in Pakistan. We have also begun taking on long-term lease and management of fifteen-odd budget hotels. Owned by others but run by one of our companies, these are branded as the 'Hotel One' chain. Generally speaking, I like running a hotel myself, not sharing that responsibility with others. A friend once asked me why. I thought for a moment and said, 'I guess I'm a hands-on person. Till I came to Dubai, I was not driven around. I liked driving myself. That's my philosophy with hotels too.'

~

This chapter has probably brought you up to date with my hotel business but has made quite a mess of chronology! I began in the 1980s but ended with my vision for a hotel chain in 2020! To make amends, I must restore the chronology and go back to where we began, the Zia era. While I did get possession of what became the first Pearl Continental hotels in the Zia period, my relations with Pakistan's military strongman remained rocky.

In 1978, I sought permission to start Indus Airways and hired Air Vice-Marshal Eric Hall, recently retired from the Pakistan Air Force, to run what would have been the country's first private airline. I was refused clearances by the government. Another company, Shaheen, was given permission. Shaheen faltered and began not with air services but bus services. With my experience in the hotel industry and insights into the tourism sector, I was confident I could have delivered an excellent product and Pakistan could have had a sizeable, professionally run private airline by now. It was not to be. Later Zia refused permission for a polyester fibre plant I wanted to set up. Our equation became quite nasty, as I have described in earlier chapters. The frost seemed to melt by the late 1980s, when Zia tried to overcome some of the mutual acrimony. Perhaps he realized he had been unfair to me. Whatever it was, he broke the ice by greeting me publicly at a wedding in Karachi.

A mutual friend, A.R. Shefta, a Pakistani who had married a Japanese woman and lived in Tokyo, also played a role in the reconciliation. Shefta used to stay in my hotels and was fond of me, though he was much older. He was also a childhood friend of Zia's. I think it was in the winter of 1987 that Shefta came on one of his regular visits to Pakistan. One day, I got a telephone call from him, asking me to reach the state guest house in Karachi as soon as possible. He gave no other details. Mystified, I drove down to the guest house and was received by Shefta at the gate. He pulled me by my arm and took me into one of the rooms. There I saw Zia, grinning his trademark grin. 'How are you, Hashwani?' he asked, as if greeting an old friend. I was taken aback but tried not to show it. 'I am fine,' I responded, 'and I am here because Shefta called me . . . Do you want to arrest me again?' Zia laughed and waved his hand: 'No, no, it wasn't me. It was Junejo.' Suddenly the memories of that humiliating period came rushing back. Rather than feel satisfied, I got emotional and a bit angry. 'Whoever did it, General sahib,' I said, 'will die a miserable death because he humiliated my beloved mother. I did not leave the country despite my arrest being imminent. I was ready to face it all. Why were my family members, particularly my ageing mother, put through torture? I was not running away.' An awkward silence followed but Shefta saved the day by putting his arm on my shoulder and saying, 'It was tough, Sadru, but forget the past. Let's move on . . .'

In the coming months, I was to meet Zia several times. It was as if he was trying to make up for declaring me persona non grata and not wanting to see my face, to borrow his own words. He would hold my hand and ask how things were, inquire about the hotels and the business. I must confess that it disconcerted me at times. I wondered what was going on. Talking about my hotels one day, I told him about the Bhurban project and how I had conceived it, sharing the story of the picnic with my daughters, the beautiful location, how it could change the local economy, all the details. He seemed genuinely interested and his eyes lit up. I asked him whether he would be willing to lay the foundation stone of the Pearl Continental Bhurban. He agreed at once. We fixed the event for 8 August 1988, and made all the arrangements for a presidential visit. A mock village was put up and an elaborate menu drawn up for lunch. On 6 August, I got a message from Zia's secretary. The previous day, Arif Hussain Hussaini, a prominent Shia leader, had been shot at and killed outside a mosque in Peshawar. Zia would have to attend his funeral, as a senior Iranian delegation was on its way. The ceremony at Bhurban would have to be postponed.

The situation was disappointing but unavoidable. I spoke to Zia's secretary and he assured me a fresh date would be finalized soon. With a heavy heart, we withdrew the invitations that had already gone out and dismantled the mock village. I decided to take my family to Bangkok and Singapore for a break, far from the stresses of work. It was a private visit, in the days before mobile phones, and I left instructions that my company executives were not to disturb me. This was time I had set aside for my children. On the morning of 18 August, I picked up the newspaper outside my hotel room in Singapore and scanned the headlines. I couldn't believe what I read. A day earlier, General Zia had died in a plane crash. A welter of thoughts overcame me. I was stunned, bewildered, confused and, for all the bitterness of the years gone by, upset. I couldn't whitewash Zia's failings—and there were so many—and his hostility towards me. Even so, Zia had been a presence in Pakistan for over a decade. Now, yet again, Pakistan was at a crossroads.

Two days later, I returned to Pakistan. Construction began in Bhurban after a low-key, subdued foundation stone ceremony. Later, a friend in military intelligence told me that those who had planned the air crash—there was widespread acceptance that it was not an accident and some have termed it the last assassination of the Cold War—may have wanted to kill Zia while he was in Bhurban on 8 August. I shuddered at the thought, and thanked the Almighty. He had saved all of us. Now the Almighty would have to save Pakistan and set it on a new path.

9

THE DECADE OF
THE CIVILIANS

In any given human framework, when an entrenched and
controlling entity collapses or is suddenly removed, there is
scope for confusion and unpredictable consequences. New
forces and energies get released and come into play, some
positive and some negative. Power alignments are redrawn.
Accepted postulates are interrogated or threatened. This is
what happened to large parts of Eastern Europe and Central
Asia, for instance, when the Communist regime in the
Soviet Union crumbled so dramatically in the beginning
of the 1990s. The world and the region, and Russia
itself as a society, are still experiencing the aftershocks
of that event. In the years following Zia's death in 1988,

something similar happened to Pakistan, but on a smaller scale. As a country and as a people, we started to discover ourselves again. It was a time of multiple changes. The dreaded dictatorial military leader was gone. The Afghan War, which had consumed so much of Pakistan's national life and so many of its human and material resources for the past decade, was ending. Those we considered our friends and had harboured, the mujahideen, had won and those we felt were our enemies, the Soviet occupiers, had been defeated. Zia's death was followed by concern and fear of the unknown but also by hope and optimism of fresh beginnings. To cite one compelling statistic: through the eleven years of Zia's rule, we waited and waited for a genuine and free election in Pakistan. In the nine years between 1988, when Zia's plane crashed, and 1997, Pakistan saw not one, not two but four general elections. In 1999, the wheel turned full circle and the army seized power again, under General Musharraf. This chapter is about the bulk of those eleven years between Zia and Musharraf, a period of two PMs (both of whom served two truncated terms) and an undulating decade of civilian politics, the longest such run in my adult life as a Pakistani.

Immediately after Zia's death was announced, Ghulam Ishaq Khan took over as President. A senior and upright civil servant and former finance minister—he had played a pivotal role, readers may recall, in the privatization of some industries in Pakistan—Ghulam Ishaq Khan had risen to the position of Chairman of the Senate (upper house of Pakistan's parliament). National elections were held in November 1988, within three months of Zia's passing. While no party won a majority in the lower house, Benazir's PPP was the single-largest party by a long way. Led by Nawaz Sharif, then an upcoming politician from Punjab, the Islami Jamhoori Ittehad (Islamic Democratic Alliance) emerged as a strong opposition. Some of us felt that, at long last, Pakistan was headed towards a two-party or bipolar political system, with competition between the centre-left and the centre-right. On being sworn in as PM, Benazir became not just the popular face of Pakistan but the star of Asia, an intelligent and quick-witted woman leader in the Islamic world. She was young and charming, having got married only the previous year. It seemed she could do no wrong.

Unfortunately, like her father, she would come to believe in her infallibility and suffer for it in due course. I first met Benazir in early 1989 at an event in Rawalpindi held in honour of His Highness Prince Karim Aga Khan, who was visiting Pakistan. That was at the start of her term but it was already becoming clear that she was not a deft and tested administrator. She had frequent disagreements with Ghulam Ishaq Khan and, finally, twenty months after she became PM, the President dismissed her government and dissolved the National Assembly (lower house of Parliament). In October 1990, fresh elections were called. The dismissal of Benazir's government was both controversial and well received. It may sound paradoxical and has to be understood in the context of the complexity of the time. Ghulam Ishaq Khan's decision to dismiss Benazir's government drew from the Eighth Amendment to the Pakistani Constitution. This was an interpolation in the Constitution that went back to Zia's years and sought to give the President overriding powers to neutralize or supplant a civilian PM. It was Zia's security blanket when he experimented with a form of controlled civilian rule and handed over some powers to a civilian PM, Mohammad Khan Junejo, in 1985. It was never expected that a titular President would use it against a popularly elected PM after democracy had been restored. Ghulam Ishaq Khan saw his role differently. He regarded the presidency as the guardian of probity and ethics in public life and as the guarantor of the last resort of the Pakistani people. He was honest but he could also be rigid and pedantic in the manner of bureaucrats. Democracy, however, is more free-floating and doesn't stay within the confines of pre-written rules. That is why politicians and norm-bound bureaucrats, with the best of intentions from both ends, sometimes just don't understand each other's universes. To some degree, this happened with Ghulam Ishaq Khan and Benazir and later with Ghulam Ishaq Khan and Nawaz Sharif as well. Both their governments were dismissed by Ghulam Ishaq Khan—Benazir's in 1990 and Nawaz Sharif's in 1993—for similar allegations. Could Ghulam Ishaq Khan have handled the situation with greater dexterity and used his influence and knowledge of the levers of power in Islamabad to put pressure on one or both of these PMs to rectify errors? I suppose one will never know.

Anyway, I am getting ahead of the story. In 1990, when Benazir was dismissed from office, there was relief that a very corrupt and very disappointing government, which had frittered away its goodwill fairly soon, was gone. Benazir's government had proved unequal to the economic challenges that Pakistan faced. Lawlessness and whimsicality, perhaps nurtured and encouraged by Benazir's inner council and by her husband, left a lasting impact on government and society.

I experienced it myself. In fact, I had to move from Karachi, the city of my birth, to Islamabad in 1990. This was not a planned migration or a business decision but an attempt to protect my family and me from criminal elements, backed by political forces out to get me in Karachi. In comparison, the national capital was too high-profile a location for my enemies to plan a daring attack on me. It would have alerted the media and the political and military establishment. The person targeting me was none

155

other than Asif Ali Zardari. As soon as his wife came to power, Zardari and his cronies pushed government officials to investigate my companies to find any evidence that Zia had done me favours. Consider the irony. A decade earlier, Zia had victimized me because he thought I had benefited from Zulfikar Ali Bhutto. Now Benazir's government was harassing me on the suspicion that I had taken undue help from Zia. While Zardari had a personal score to settle with me, given our past history in Karachi and the disco incident in 1983 (*see* chapter 7), he was also doing this with other businessmen and resourceful individuals because he saw his wife's electoral victory as not just a political but also a commercial opportunity. Friends and those civil servants who knew me were aghast. Far from being an ally of the earlier regime, I had suffered under Zia and was, by a new twist of fate, suspected of having PPP sympathies. Yet, Zardari urged for a probe trying to find incriminating documents against me that, well, just didn't exist. Well-wishers began to warn me that I wasn't quite a favourite of the government's, though they couldn't understand why. When the PM invited leading businessmen to discuss Pakistan's economy and commercial climate, I was deliberately excluded. Zardari was probably waiting for me to turn up at his door but I wasn't going to.

One day, Zardari called me. Many years earlier, I had bought a plot of land in Karachi from a Parsi family. 'I want to buy that land,' Zardari said to me. 'I have a project under construction adjacent to this plot. If I can add this land to the project area, it will be a big help.' I agreed to sell. He asked, 'How much did you pay for it?' 'I bought it years ago, at the correct price then,' I said. Attempting to be diplomatic, I offered to sell it to him for my purchase price, even though the value had shot up in the intervening years and the market price was much higher. Zardari was not satisfied. When he came home to finalize the deal, I could tell that he wanted me to hand it over for free. I ignored the signals. I had no desire to give him the land as a gift and a bribe and then wait for him to do me favours using public money. That was not the way I did business. I sold the plot at my cost price. The whole experience of meeting and selling that piece of land to Zardari was unpleasant. It gave me a good idea of his greed and character.

Meanwhile, life carried on. On 22 December 1989, I lost my dear mother. I was shattered by her death. Both my parents were gone, my favourite brother, Hasan Ali, was dead. I had strained relations with my elder brother Akbar. I felt lonely. I was fortunate that the Pakistan Army corps commander in Karachi at the time was General Asif Nawaz Janjua, a very, very close friend. A fine man and a thoroughly professional soldier—among the best in Pakistan's history—Asif Nawaz later became Chief of the Pakistan Army. In 1990, General Asif Nawaz saved me from great danger. The story merits retelling and offers a window into the murky world and the conspiracies that even ordinary businessmen have to encounter in Pakistan. It was a few weeks after my mother's death that I noticed that my car was being followed. Every morning as I drove myself to work, or later in the day to meetings or social occasions, I was being tailed. A little perturbed, I began to take along a bodyguard in the car, seated in the passenger seat, next to me. Still, strange men seemed to hang around me, make efforts to come close to me and strike up conversations or even visit my office under some pretext, apparently looking for a job or asking for directions or making small talk with colleagues. One afternoon, I got a telephone call from a banker friend. After exchanging pleasantries, he told me something that took me aback. 'Hashwani sahib, you will remember that you have kept the share documents of Pakistan Services Limited in the lockers of the United Bank of Pakistan,' he said. 'Please take them away and put them elsewhere. There is an evil eye on them.' The message was cryptic but sent a chill down my spine. PSL was the flagship company that owned the Pearl Continental chain. The shares had been pledged with United Bank and loans taken against them. Obviously, somebody in power and influence was planning to use those shares to try and effect a takeover or claim that I had not paid interest and seize the shares or perhaps just make the shares disappear. It would be absolutely illegal but would cause me immense problems and send me into endless rounds of litigation. Immediately, I repaid United Bank, took possession of the share documents, and put them in safe custody in another bank, where political interference was less likely.

These events were starting to make me uneasy. I guessed Zardari was somehow connected to all of it but was unsure. In any case, he was the PM's husband and the most powerful man in the country. What could I do? One day, I was having lunch with Rafi Raza, a well-known barrister and constitutional expert and minister from the Zulfikar Ali Bhutto years who had subsequently moved to London. It was a long and leisurely lunch as we were meeting after several months and had much to talk about. As we left the restaurant, I virtually ran to my car and drove quickly to the Cotton Exchange building, which housed my office. As I walked in, I was told that some people had been waiting to see me for three hours. I was a bit surprised because no such meeting had been planned. As I climbed up to the first floor, I saw three men. I couldn't tell who they were. One was a swarthy man, wearing sunglasses indoors. I couldn't see his eyes and this disconcerted me—I like to look people in the eye to read their intentions. I felt distinctly uncomfortable. My hair was standing on edge . . . Something was amiss. 'What can I do for you?' I asked in Sindhi. 'We have come to seek a donation from you,' said the man in the dark glasses, 'for an event to be held in Mehran University on 19 January [1990].' I was perplexed but responded at once, 'I can give you a cheque today. If you want cash, please come back tomorrow.' 'Okay,' the man said, 'we'll come tomorrow.' As they walked out, they handed me an invitation card to the event.

I went to my desk and read the card. It was an invitation to an event to be presided over by P.K. Shahani, a senior PPP functionary and civil rights activist. Shahani, an accomplished chartered surveyor, was an adviser to one of our companies and received a retainer from us. I felt a little reassured. Perhaps Shahani had sent them. My suspicions were soon restored though. As the three men had left my office, I had signalled to an office assistant to follow them. He came back and reported that he walked behind them for a few minutes and heard them say to each other, 'He's the man . . .' I telephoned Shahani and requested him to come over immediately. When I showed him the card, he said it was a forgery—there was no such event at Mehran University. I was alarmed and immediately called up friends in the police. They took down descriptions of the three men and came to the conclusion that the man in the dark glasses was Bashir Qureshi and one of the other two was his sidekick, Laghari. They were noted criminals, part of the broader Jiye Sindh movement, which had begun as a sociopolitical platform to promote Sindhi identity but had soon been corrupted by unwanted elements and rowdy students who turned to crime and extortion. Bashir was known to be the most aggressive of this brigade.

The men did not return the following day but I was worried. A sense of captivity engulfed me. I felt I was under constant surveillance. I consulted General Asif Nawaz who advised me to change my route to and from work every day and to increase security at home and work. I did so but a sense of foreboding and the feeling that I was being tracked refused to disappear. I had a premonition that something major, something nasty was about to happen. I bought tickets for my children and made plans to send them to Dubai and then London on 14 January. I told nobody about this but prepared to end *chehlum*, the period of mourning for my mother, in twenty-one days rather than the traditional forty. On the evening of 13 January, I told my family to start packing. On the morning of 14 January, with only hours to go for my children and me to fly out, I got a call from General Asif Nawaz. It was not even 8 a.m. but he was clearly agitated. 'Come to my office in thirty minutes,' he said, 'but don't take the usual route to the corps headquarters. Take some other route . . . Be careful.' Twenty-five minutes later he telephoned again. I hadn't left the house and he was upset that I was late. 'Hurry up,' he said, before hanging up.

When I reached the corps headquarters, members of General Asif Nawaz's personal staff were waiting for me at the gate. They took me to his room, where I met senior officers of the Mehran Force, a unit of the Pakistan Army tasked with internal security duties in Sindh. (The Mehran Force is now part of the Pakistan Rangers of Sindh.) I was shown a letter that commanders of the Mehran Force had written to the Government of Sindh, asking that I be given security as I was being targeted by kidnappers. Qureshi and Laghari had been released from prison two weeks earlier. When they came to know about this, the Mehran Force officers—who had been assigned the job of fighting crime and lawlessness in Karachi and Sindh—knew something was afoot. They contacted Qaim Ali Shah, the chief minister of Sindh. He had no idea that Qureshi had been released. The following day, Qaim Ali Shah had got back and told General Asif Nawaz that the two had been freed on orders from Islamabad. It was apparent they were being geared for a special mission. The army activated its informers and found out Qureshi and Laghari had been contracted to abduct and kill Sadruddin Hashwani. The plot details were revealed to me. On 19 January, as I left Bath Island, my car would be blocked, my guards shot, and I taken away. Then I would be forced to sign papers giving away my properties, particularly my hotels, to others, and thrown into the Indus.

At this point, General Asif Nawaz spoke. 'You have to leave,' he said. 'We have decided against sending you to Islamabad, as we can't predict what Zardari will do. I suggest you leave for Lahore. I have already spoken to Nawaz Sharif to offer you protection.' Nawaz Sharif was then the chief minister of Punjab. I said I was grateful and could now make sense of the crowd around me, constantly keeping an eye on my movements. Rather than Lahore, however, I wanted to fly overseas. I said, 'I have already booked myself on the 4 p.m. flight to Dubai. My children are coming with me. I will take them to London and enrol them in boarding schools.' Escorted by soldiers in uniform, I went home and then left for the airport. The ride to the airport and the security protocol are etched in my memory. There were two trucks with soldiers in front of our cars and two trucks with soldiers behind our cars. There were military escorts on either side as well. In the following days, I admitted Hasan Ali to Millfield, the school in Surrey where my older boy Murtaza was already studying. Hasan Ali was twelve and Millfield usually took in children once they turned thirteen. I persuaded the headmaster to make an exception as Hasan Ali was only a few months short of thirteen. Next, I took Nadia and Shazia, my two older daughters, to a boarding school in Switzerland. Sarah was too young, however. Back in London, I rented an apartment in Park Lane area and stayed there, having been advised by General Asif Nawaz to keep away from Karachi.

Three months later, things looked better. Rumours that Zardari had plotted to kidnap and kill a leading businessman of Pakistan had spread. Also, General Asif Nawaz had been promoted as chief of general staff—a step below the position of army chief—and posted to Rawalpindi, where the Pakistan Army headquarters is situated. He advised me to relocate from Karachi and settle permanently in Islamabad. In the national capital, so close to other centres of power, including the civil service, the army and the diplomatic community, Zardari would perhaps be cautious. I rented a house in Islamabad. Shortly afterwards, my eldest daughter, Nadia, got married and moved to Islamabad with her husband, living in a house close by. I continued to visit London and finally bought a short lease on an apartment in Hans Place, near Harrods, so that the boys could 'come home' every weekend from Surrey. About two years later, I moved Hasan Ali from Millfield (he didn't like it there) and enrolled him in the well-known Swiss school Le Rosey. Sarah also joined him. For a year, I visited them regularly, worried and upset that they were so far away from home and were not growing up in Pakistan, in a milieu that was their own. I lidn't want them to become cultural misfits in Pakistan. About a year later, I brought Hasan Ali and Sarah back to Pakistan and admitted them to the American School in Islamabad. They were ensured a good, world-class education and could spend time with me in Pakistan. Murtaza, who was still in Millfield, went to the US to pursue higher studies. Meanwhile, I settled in Islamabad, eventually buying a plot of land and building a house there. The land I bought, and the older house on it, had belonged to General Ayub Khan. His family had sold it to the Punjab Tourism Corporation, from which I bought it. The house I built is still my home in Islamabad.

~

In August 1990, Ghulam Ishaq Khan used his presidential powers to dismiss the Benazir government. Fresh elections were called for in November 1990, wherein an alliance led by Nawaz Sharif won. I had known Nawaz Sharif somewhat. He was the son of a respected businessman and was always courteous to me. I found him a practical man, free of the bookish theories of socialism and of the Bhutto rhetoric, more in tune with the economic problems, potentials and aspirations of Pakistanis. To be fair, Nawaz Sharif's first term in office—he was PM from 1990 to 1993, before being dismissed by Ghulam Ishaq Khan—was very productive for Pakistan. He appointed General Asif Nawaz Janjua as Chief of Army Staff and focused on the economy and what he called his National Economic Reconstruction Programme. A rapid privatization initiative was announced. This was the first major effort in Pakistan to dramatically reverse Bhutto's nationalization binge of the early 1970s. Private sector investment, industrialization, power and highway projects, and ambitious reforms and deregulation were all on the agenda. It was the most business-friendly policy environment I had known in Pakistan. I was very happy—for myself and for my country.

By then, I was a part of Islamabad's social set. The Marriott Hotel had given me a standing in local society. I had a high profile and knew everybody worth knowing: ministers, civil servants, business executives, diplomats. After all, all major social events from weddings to conferences would be held at the Marriott, the only hotel of any reckoning in Islamabad. During this period, Benazir, then an Opposition leader, came to my house for tea. She was accompanied by senior party colleagues, including Farooq Leghari, who later became President of Pakistan. Zardari was conspicuously absent. I have still not been able to understand whether Benazir knew what her husband had been up to in Karachi and the extent of his conspiracy against me. Perhaps her visit was a way of asking me to forget the past.

The year 1993 began on a bad note with the death of General Asif Nawaz. To say that I was stunned would be an understatement. On 3 January, I was part of a small group of immediate family and friends who had gathered to celebrate General Asif Nawaz's fifty-sixth birthday. We sang 'Happy birthday to you' and I wished him a long life. He brushed it aside with a smile, saying: 'Don't wish me such things.' I was left uneasy by that remark but soon forgot about it. He had proved to be an exemplary general. He had supported democracy and refused to entertain ideas of a coup or to intervene in politics. He had made it plain that he saw the army as an upstanding institution that had the best interests of Pakistan at heart, and resorted to blunt speaking with politicians. This earned him many enemies. On 8 January, he suffered a heart attack while jogging and died. This struck many of us as being odd. After all, he was a physically fit person, with no serious illnesses. It was widely suspected that he had been poisoned and, to this day, the mystery of General Asif Nawaz's death persists. When his hair was sent for forensic examination, a very high level of arsenic was found. He was lost to Pakistan and to his family—and to me personally—way too early.

General Asif Nawaz was succeeded by General Abdul Waheed Kakar, another fine soldier. By now, the air in Islamabad was thick with conspiracy. In April 1993, President Ghulam Ishaq Khan dismissed Nawaz Sharif and precipitated a constitutional crisis. General Kakar stepped in and gave wise behind-the-scenes counsel. He prevailed upon both Ghulam Ishaq Khan and Nawaz Sharif to resign. A fresh election was the only solution. Voting took place in October 1993. It was a very tightly fought election. The PPP won 89 seats out of 207 and the Pakistan Muslim League (Nawaz) or PML (N) won 73, though it had a slightly higher share of the popular vote. Benazir was able to cobble together a coalition and become PM for the second time. We hoped that she had learnt from the mistakes of her first term and matured into a seasoned politician. Certainly, she was careful in her dealings with and public utterances about the army in the early months of her second stint. Since Ghulam Ishaq Khan had left the presidency, she chose Farooq Leghari, a non-controversial and academically oriented Baloch leader of the PPP, as President. She made all the right noises about economic growth and development and job creation and promised to sustain and continue Nawaz Sharif's economic reforms and privatization programme. In practice, this did not happen with the gusto that was needed. The left-wing foundations of the PPP and its age-old suspicion of private enterprise were difficult to dislodge. When it came to the denationalization of Pakistan Railway and Pakistan Steel Mills, Benazir refused to go ahead. The economy began to suffer and investor confidence dried up. That aside, internal security challenges were mounting and

Benazir was unable to quell violence in Karachi as well as Lahore. In Karachi, part of the problem was Zardari, who saw himself as the uncrowned overlord of Sindh. Major corruption scandals, including bribes in the purchase of submarines from a French company, surfaced and Zardari came to be universally despised as 'Mr Ten Per Cent'. The submarine scandal later led to his arrest and trial. Trying to please all sides at all times, Benazir allowed herself to be persuaded to intervene in politics in Afghanistan and arm the Taliban militia, believing that it would do Pakistan's bidding. It is for history to judge whether this was an astute move or if keeping an arm's length and letting the various political factions in Afghanistan decide for themselves may have been better. The mid-1990s were terrible years for Pakistan and severely tarnished Benazir's reputation. She was also fighting family battles against her brother Murtaza, who saw himself as a rival for the Bhutto family's political legacy. Murtaza was a hothead and, like Zardari, not averse to using guns to achieve political objectives. The two men emerged as foes—when Murtaza was shot and killed by the police in Karachi on 20 September 1996, his brother-in-law's indirect role was suspected. The killing of Murtaza Bhutto was the final nail in the coffin. The charges of corruption, the economic meltdown, the general disgust with the Benazir government peaked. Within two months, Farooq

Leghari—Benazir's hand-picked President—used the Eighth Amendment to dismiss her government. Benazir was stunned at what she considered Leghari's 'betrayal' but most neutral observers were just glad. Her government had been very disappointing and, once more, she had let Zardari run amok.

In the three years before this debacle, I had come to know Benazir better. In public, she was respectful and polite. At one point, she offered me a senator's position and asked me to join her government as an economic adviser. I said I was touched but would have to decline. I had my business to look after, and was not interested in politics. Besides, I was embarking on a new adventure by entering the oil and gas sector, and that was consuming my time. I did not ask Benazir for any favours, ensuring her my commitment was to Pakistan, irrespective of who was in power. However, Zardari continued to see me as a thorn. I applied for permission to build a 250-MW power plant but the PPP government refused to clear the project. The government invited offers to build a new five-star hotel in Karachi, right by the sea. I put in what I felt was a strong bid. After a few days, I got a telephone call from Zardari. He wanted to give the hotel project to his friend Tufail 'Tony' Shaikh, a Karachi-based businessman. I understood the message and withdrew my bid. What else could I do? Zardari is still around, Tufail Shaikh is still around, that plot of land is still around. The hotel hasn't come up to this day. Of course, in neither case did I go to Benazir to complain. She must have known what was going on but was unwilling or unable to stop her husband. To me, it was apparent that he was a petty man. Once I met Zardari after he had returned from a tour of several countries, travelling with the PM. I asked him to relate his experiences of meeting so many international leaders. Who had impressed him and why? His answer astounded me: 'They are all stupid and below average . . . No understanding of ground realities.' He was so dismissive. I was amazed.

After Benazir was removed as PM in November 1996, President Leghari appointed Malik Meraj Khalid, a senior and unassuming politician, as caretaker PM. This was a period of churning in Pakistan. The economy, internal peace, foreign relations—all were in turmoil. Popular anger against Benazir was very intense. People were feeling let down. In February 1997, elections were held and the results were there for all to see. The PML (N) won an overwhelming 137 seats of the 207 for which polling was held. The PPP was reduced to a rump of only 18 seats. The people had taught Benazir and, perhaps more than her, Zardari a lesson. As her husband continued to be accused of corruption and wrongdoing and had legal cases hurled at him, Benazir left Pakistan with her children in 1998 and settled in Dubai. She was not to return home for a decade and when she did so, in October 2007, it was to be tragically assassinated.

~

Nawaz Sharif's second term did not begin on a good note for me. Some people had poisoned his ears and convinced him that I had benefited from the PPP patronage, which was quite contrary to the truth. I was in Houston when my office told me I had yet again been placed on the Exit Control List. Immediately, I flew back to Islamabad, becoming the only person in the history of Pakistan to return to the country from overseas despite being put on the Exit Control List. I arrived on 14 March 1997, and invited Nicholas Platt home for dinner the following evening. Platt, who had served as US ambassador to Pakistan in the early 1990s, was visiting Islamabad in his capacity as chairman of the Asia Society. He was an old friend and I had planned nothing more than a light, conversational evening. Platt had more serious questions on his mind. As soon as he sat down in my living room, he asked, 'Why is Nawaz so hostile to you? I thought the two of you got along famously.' I shrugged my shoulders—I was surprised myself. 'I'm having breakfast with him tomorrow in Murree,' Platt added. 'Do you want me to talk to him?' I shook my head. 'Please don't. I have no issues with him. I am sure it's a minor misunderstanding and will sort itself out.' Yet, something had obviously gone quite wrong. Friends in the bureaucracy told me that Nawaz Sharif had somehow been given the impression that I was cultivating a political role. I received an income tax notice. The Pakistan International Airlines in-flight catering contract with our hotels was abruptly terminated. Crew members staying in our hotels were moved elsewhere. My business rivals were at work again. I tried to meet the PM to clarify any doubts he may have but was not given an appointment. Saifur Rehman was appointed chairman of the National Accountability Bureau (NAB) (Ehtesab Bureau), an anti-corruption watchdog agency, and asked to investigate controversial deals of the Benazir–Zardari regime. Apparently, he was also asked to make inquiries into my business transactions. A stream of inspectors and investigators began coming to my offices and hotels, in some cases asking for photocopies of bills and receipts that were several years old.

All of this started to happen within days of my return to Pakistan. One morning, I got a telephone call from Rafat Mahdi, additional secretary in the ministry of foreign affairs. Mahdi, who later served Pakistan as ambassador to the European Union, was a good man and a sober diplomat. The summit meeting of the Organization of Islamic Conference was to take place in Islamabad on

23 and 24 March, he said, and little had been arranged. He had been told to set things right 'without involving Hashwani's hotels, as these were under investigation'. The poor man didn't know what to do. Some 1800 visitors were arriving in Pakistan within a week, but accommodation and logistics had not been arranged. Mahdi spoke to Nawaz Sharif and bluntly told him it was impossible to achieve all this without using the facilities of the Marriott and the Hashoo Group. Reluctantly, Nawaz Sharif agreed. Mahdi met me at the Marriott that afternoon—a few hours after his call—and was clearly worried. 'In the name of Pakistan, I request you to please help me organize this conference successfully. Without your help, the conference may as well go to some other country. We will lose face.' There was no question of not helping. 'All my hotels,' I said, 'the Marriott in Islamabad, the Pearl Continental in Rawalpindi, and the Pearl Continental in Bhurban, are at your disposal. That's 700 rooms.' Mahdi nodded but didn't smile, 'I need more,' he said. 'I need 1800 rooms. I want you to take over the MNA [Member of the National Assembly] hostel, which has 300 rooms, Punjab House, Sindh House, the Ministers' Colony houses, the convention centre and manage all these . . . housekeeping, food, everything.' The MNA hostel and convention centre had just been built. They were brand new but nobody knew what problems were hidden in them—in terms of water and electricity lines,

leakages and seepages, and so on. I threw up my hands. 'Rafat,' I said, 'I don't have Aladdin's lamp . . .' 'The choice is yours,' he retorted. 'Do you want Pakistan's image to be saved or to be destroyed?' There was no choice. 'You have placed such a burden on my head,' I said, '. . . but Pakistan comes first. We will do it, somehow we will do it.' It was a massive exercise. In two days, we moved 400 people from our hotels in other cities, like Karachi and Peshawar, to Islamabad. The hostel rooms and other government buildings were scrubbed clean, food arrangements made, bedrooms upgraded to five-star levels. Upholstery, bed linen, bathroom fittings, and general interiors were focused on minutely. By all accounts, the conference was the most successful in Pakistan's history.

I wasn't even sent an invitation.

Even after the conference, I continued to be harassed. Twenty-two telephone lines that were in my name were tapped and bank accounts blocked. I was told I'd be arrested for allegedly manipulating the auctions of some pieces of land in conjunction with Shafi Siwani, chairman of the Capital Development Authority in Islamabad. This was nonsense. In all my life, I had never gone to a land auction. One Saturday, my youngest, Sarah, telephoned me at work and said there was a posse of black cars driving around our house. The following Monday, General Jehangir Karamat, who had become army chief in January 1996 and was also a trusted friend, called me to the Army House in Rawalpindi. 'Sadru,' he said, 'some people are out to fix you. Do you want me to speak to the PM?' I thanked him but declined. 'My hands are clean,' I said, 'and it will end sooner or later.' 'Okay, your choice,' General Karamat said, 'but call me if you need help.' Five days later, I was told that criminal charges had been filed against Siwani and my name had been added as a suspected co-conspirator. I was to be arrested that very evening. I went home, packed some clothes and essential medicines, and left Islamabad before sunset. The police had planned to arrest me after sunset to avoid taking me to court the same day. I drove through the night, crossing Punjab. For a month, I lived in tribal areas such as Charsadda. I would change my location every four or five days. It was physical and mental torture. My sons would contact me using a Thuraya satellite phone, to escape surveillance by the government. Those were gruelling days and nights. In a strange, dark and silent room, I would ask myself whether it was worth living in Pakistan or if I should just leave and settle elsewhere. I dismissed the thought soon enough. Generations of my family had lived in Pakistan. Nobody was going to force me to leave my own country. I am a fighter, I told myself, not a quitter.

Finally, I was granted anticipatory bail and could surface after forty days in hiding, on the run. I was served a notice to appear in Lahore High Court for bail confirmation.

I landed in Lahore at 8.30 p.m. from Islamabad. To my shock, the airport lounge was full of intelligence and police officials. They followed me to the Pearl Continental Hotel and placed policemen outside my room. At 8 a.m. the next morning I left for the court, a cavalcade of intelligence and police cars following me. The High Court premises too were crowded with such officials. I was told that the judge was under pressure to refuse confirmation of my bail. My lawyer, Akram Sheikh, was pessimistic. 'I don't think I can help you today, Mr Hashwani,' he told me. 'He will not confirm your bail and they will arrest you in court itself!' It was a minor matter concerning confirmation of bail but the advocate-general of Pakistan, no less, was sitting in court, bolstering the prosecution and preparing to appear himself. As Akram Sheikh began to speak, I went outside for some fresh air and a moment of peace. I looked to the sky and prayed, begging Allah for help, pleading for mercy. A few minutes later, I was summoned. The advocate-general had suddenly left the courtroom and as there was nobody else to press for cancellation, my bail was confirmed. It was a miracle. I had tears in my eyes. This turned the tide. The cases against me began to fall to pieces. In a few months, I was cleared of all charges. My innocence had been vindicated.

In the days that followed, I often thought of what had happened. One question rankled me. A decade had passed since Zia's death, a decade of democratic and civilian rule. Why had it proved so disappointing? Why did civilian rulers take so long to do what was obviously the right thing? Why were civilian politicians so reluctant to serve the interests of the people who had elected them? These issues continued to haunt me as we entered 1998. In the summer of that year, the need for resolve and firm leadership in Pakistan was to acquire an altogether different meaning, as our country faced an existential threat. More of that, and of my role in pushing Pakistan towards nuclear tests, in the following chapter.

10

BATTLE FATIGUES

In May 1998, India conducted five nuclear tests and declared itself a nuclear power. It was a moment of truth for Pakistan, and it was clear as daylight to all patriotic Pakistanis that our country had to do likewise and go ahead with nuclear tests of its own. Even so, for a few exasperating weeks, the Nawaz Sharif government demurred. Public officials called for internal debate. Newspapers conducted opinion polls. Economists, even some of my fellow businessmen, warned of Western economic sanctions and short- to medium-term damage to the economy and individual businesses, especially those dependent on international buyers or customers. Without disagreeing that there would be consequences to a nuclear test, I must say I was dumbfounded. I do not consider myself a hawk or a warmonger, and I sincerely hope I live to see the day when no country has nuclear weapons and universal disarmament has been achieved. Nevertheless, it was apparent to me that India, the country that posed the greatest strategic threat to Pakistan and with which we had fought three wars, had just given itself a huge advantage via nuclear weapons. This advantage would have to be neutralized—it was as simple as that. The decision had been forced upon us. National security and the public's anxiety necessitated nuclear tests. There was just no alternative.

Yet, many politicians seemed to waver. A stream of American visitors—officials from Washington DC and others who had influence in Pakistan—arrived and promised aid to Pakistan if it didn't test. I was upset. Speaking to friends one evening, I was openly critical of the government's inability to come to a quick decision. 'Will we not test and will we mortgage our national security,' I exclaimed, 'just because somebody offers us a few million dollars?' In any case, the money would never reach the poor. It would be eaten up by politicians and bureaucrats. Unfortunately, leading businessmen in Pakistan ducked the issue and refused to take a strong position. In the meantime, the Indian reaction was one of jubilation and jingoism. On 18 May, India's home minister, L.K. Advani, visited the part of Kashmir that is under Indian control and made threatening noises. He said India had 'resolved to deal firmly with Pakistan's hostile activities' and would 'not shy away from our strengths'. He argued the 'decisive step to become a nuclear weapon state has brought about a qualitative new state in India–Pakistan relations, particularly in finding a lasting solution to the Kashmir problem'. He warned Pakistan to accept the 'change in the geo-strategic situation in the region' and was explicit that 'any other course will be futile and costly for Pakistan'. In fact, there was a steady stream of such crude and celebratory statements coming out of India, and among Indian expatriates. I could guess the impact it was having on ordinary citizens in Pakistan as well as on the overseas Pakistani community. I spoke to friends in the army. What they had to say worried me even more. Morale in the military was slipping. If Pakistan did not test, ordinary soldiers, the brave men who put life and limb at risk for Pakistan, would feel let down and would feel India had gained the upper hand.

At this stage, I decided I needed to do something myself and addressed the media, urging—almost demanding— that the government carry out nuclear tests. Yes, in the immediate future, this could hurt our economy and even the Hashoo Group, but that was irrelevant when compared with the larger picture and the all-pervasive national interest. My intervention was front-page news in major newspapers and the first instance of a high-profile civilian Pakistani, outside the world of politics, making a robust case for nuclear tests in that harsh summer of 1998. Two days later, when an American delegation arrived in Islamabad, they were given photocopies of news clippings that reported my views. They were told that what I had said was representative of public pressure in Pakistan. The Americans were shocked. They had expected a businessman to play safe and caution the government, rather than push it towards nuclear tests. An acquaintance from the US embassy contacted me and expressed surprise. 'Mr Hashwani,' he said, 'we regarded you as a moderate. Why are you insistent that your government tests?' 'My friend,' I replied, 'I am not in love with nuclear weapons, but if our national interest, security and well-being demand that we have them, then we must. I am a proud Pakistani. If Pakistan doesn't survive, nothing else is worth it.' I made it clear that I was not advocating war with India, not at all. I believed in keeping one's neighbour, particularly a hostile neighbour, at arm's length. If Pakistan had a nuclear arsenal to match India's, a balance of power would be restored and we would be protected from possible Indian adventurism. Nuclear weapons have achieved such a parity—a 'balance of terror', as some analysts call it—in other parts of the world, in Europe and between the US and Russia. I was confident it could happen between Pakistan and India as well. Indeed, this is exactly what did occur. In the final week of May 1998, Pakistan conducted its nuclear tests. Since then, prospects of a large-scale war in South Asia have receded. Both sides realize the danger of escalation.

After Pakistan's tests, there was relief and euphoria among the people. I knew that the Americans and their allies would impose economic sanctions but hoped that Nawaz Sharif would use the spirit of national unity to push ahead with the much-needed economic reforms and propel Pakistanis towards rebuilding their country. Unfortunately, the government's first response was panic. Incorrectly advised by the finance minister, Sartaj Aziz, the government froze dollar-denominated bank accounts of Pakistanis and placed restrictions on the outflow of foreign exchange. More than the tests themselves, it was measures such as these that got people anxious. Instead of a sense of pride at what our nuclear scientists had achieved, a depression set in. Nevertheless, we were now a nuclear power, and the extremist voices in India hurriedly quietened down. As the dust settled, many people came to appreciate my role in the debate prior to Pakistan's tests. There was acceptance that I had thought for the country before thinking for my businesses. Gradually, Nawaz Sharif began to greet me in public. While I remained on the Exit Control List till his final day in office, personal interaction resumed.

A few weeks after the nuclear tests, differences emerged between the civilian and military leadership. Once more, it was a case of misunderstanding and suspicion, heightened by sycophants, particularly in the political establishment. A competent and professional soldier, General Karamat had no desire to restrict the functioning of the elected government. Yet, he was conscious that, as the most stable internal institution in the country, the army had a unique role to play in Pakistan, particularly in foreign policy. He spoke to the PM about institutionalizing the army's role in strategic decision-making and taking its advice in a structured manner, without impinging on the autonomy of the civilian government. This was on the lines of the role of the military in Turkey, another modern Muslim democracy. The Turkish model has been a subject of discussion in Pakistan for many years. It seems General Karamat's suggestion was misread. Urged by his advisers, Nawaz Sharif asked the general to step down in October 1998. General Karamat was an honourable man and demitted office without a fuss. If he had had any ulterior motive, he would have resisted. Instead, he chose to fade away and concentrate on his academic career. Years later, in 2004, he responded to a call to serve his country as ambassador to the US and did so to the best of his ability. Looking back, I do feel his dismissal was the turning point in Nawaz Sharif's second term as PM. He compounded the blunder by superseding two other generals and appointing General Pervez Musharraf as Chief of Army Staff. A year down the line, in October 1999, the antagonism between Nawaz Sharif and Musharraf became insurmountable. This time, the military chief did not back down gracefully—he carried out a coup. Pakistan's decade of democracy was over. We were back under a form of martial law.

I had met Musharraf socially but didn't know him very well. He had a reputation for being vindictive but also for being a clear-headed thinker. Perhaps he would take pragmatic steps, I thought. These hopes were soon belied when he appointed Lieutenant-General Mohammad Amjad, a sadistic, thoughtless general, as chairman of NAB. One of General Amjad's targets was Sadruddin Hashwani. He was determined to make an example of me on the basis of residual cases and investigations from the Nawaz Sharif era—cases that were unfounded in the first place. In fact, the Musharraf administration hired a detective agency in New York City and asked it to investigate my business affairs and investments overseas. The agency pocketed a handsome fee but found nothing incriminating. General Amjad took pleasure in humiliating those under investigation. He boasted to associates that he would make millionaires 'sleep on the floor'. This was not an honest inquiry but an ideological vendetta. When I was summoned by NAB, General Amjad made every effort to humiliate me.

On several occasions, I was reminded of the inquiry carried out by Brigadier Tajamul Hussain in the early years of the Zia period (*see* chapter 6). Brigadier Hussain and Lieutenant-General Amjad seemed to be cut from the same cloth. As stated earlier, I was part of a consortium in the US that invested in hotels and other properties. The money I made was duly remitted to Pakistan. Some of it was used, as per the rules, to pay for my children's education abroad. There was absolutely nothing covert or illegal about this. One day, I was called before NAB and almost heckled by General Amjad. In front of fifty-odd people, he began shouting. 'You are such a failure as a businessman,' he said, loudly and rudely. 'Why should anybody join you overseas? What is this consortium?' This was ridiculous. I was an internationally recognized businessman, the highest individual taxpayer in Pakistan at the time—and a mad general was going to sit in judgement over my business acumen and dismiss me as a failure! I was sharp in my retort: 'Who has given you the authority to raise a dirty finger against me? I am an honourable, successful and respected businessman.' General Amjad was not used to people standing up to him. 'I will sort you out,' he said, scowling. 'Do what you want,' I shot back, losing my inhibitions now. 'I have taken more tear gas in my youth than you have taken oxygen!'

In the days that followed, General Amjad went out of his way to implicate me. He was desperate to see me behind bars. Ironically, he also began to misuse his position as NAB chief. The anti-corruption watchdog was corrupting itself! Deals were fixed through touts and cases closed after payment of bribes. I too was approached by some middlemen. They offered to 'settle things' between General Amjad and me. I brushed them off. I remember telling one such 'agent' of General Amjad's: 'These people are not accountable today but one day they will be buried six feet below the ground, and their souls will be accountable to Allah.' Eventually, I was cleared of all charges and survived General Amjad's onslaught. The episode left me disappointed with the calibre of people in our public institutions. The best, most educated Pakistanis were not entering politics and seeking parliamentary office. In the military, men like General Amjad had risen to become three-star generals. How was this possible? How did incompetent, undeserving people get so far in our system? Islam warns its adherents against intoxication and addiction. This is usually considered a warning against alcohol and drugs. I believe it also cautions us from being intoxicated with power. That is exactly what happened to General Amjad and many of his colleagues working under Musharraf. A man who did not understand business and was corrupt to boot had set about destroying the foundations of Pakistani commerce. It left me very saddened.

~

Two years after Musharraf seized power, an event changed his life. The event made him an international celebrity and stalwart ally of the West. The event also crippled Pakistan. I am referring, of course, to 9/11, the attack on the Twin Towers of the World Trade Center in New York City on 11 September 2001. It was Tuesday evening in Pakistan and I was in the coffee shop of Marriott Islamabad. A journalist called me on my cellphone, gave me a garbled version of events, and told me to switch on the TV. I went to the GM's room and switched to CNN. One building was on fire, the result of a plane crashing into it. Initially, I thought it was an accident. Then I saw the second plane approach the other tower, take a turn, find the right angle and go straight in! This was no accident. The manner in which the pilot took a sharp turn reminded me of my younger days, when I was fascinated by sports cars. To take sharp turns with a sports car, at high speed, is a skilled art. To do it with a plane requires even greater expertise. I felt this was a military pilot. Soon media reports said those who piloted the planes on 9/11 had undergone only a few weeks of training at flying schools. This surprised me. One could not have taken those sharp turns with just a few weeks of training. It left me with the thought—shared by many others—that perhaps we still don't know the full story behind the 9/11 conspiracy.

Within minutes of the second tower being attacked, there was news of the Pentagon being damaged. By now the GM's office was packed with people. I got up, shook my head, and left. The tragedy unfolding before my eyes—the thousands of lives that would be lost in New York, a lovely and vibrant city in which I had spent such happy times—was not something I could take. More than that, I had a hunch that Pakistan would be sucked in. The suspicion would immediately be directed at Islamist groups and a pretext would be found to persecute Muslim youth, whether in Palestine or in Kashmir. Once again, the US war machine would start whirring, like it did when it bombed Hiroshima and Nagasaki in 1945, when it invaded Vietnam in 1965, and when it made Pakistan the launch pad for war in Afghanistan in the 1980s. I prayed for the souls of those who had died, and for peace. My mind told me peace was not going to be easy to achieve. Having said that, I must confess I was appalled when, in a matter of hours, Musharraf succumbed to President George W. Bush's senseless 'with us or against us' sloganeering and offered Pakistan's services as a facilitator and staging ground for the US assault on Afghanistan. There was no internal consultation, no consideration for domestic opinion, no thought for what this meant for Pakistan. Just like that, a superstar general handed over a country to the superguns of the superpower. I was distraught. How was this our war? Why was Pakistan surrendering itself once more to a superpower's agenda? An earlier general had made us suffer in the 1980s—now history was repeating itself. In the 1980s, Zia said he was helping the Americans secure freedom for Afghans. In the process, he made Pakistanis themselves less secure and less free. In 2001, Musharraf offered Pakistan's services for America's so-called war on terror. I had no doubt that we ordinary Pakistanis would pay the cost yet again.

The conflict in Afghanistan since 2001 has proven to be a very unpopular war in Pakistan. When I say this, people often misconstrue my words. I have no sympathy for terrorism and have suffered personally due to terror strikes. I have nothing but the greatest consideration for all those good people—fine, honest Americans and citizens of other countries—killed on 9/11. Yet, the greatest price for that event has been paid by Pakistan. The US lost a few thousand on 9/11. In Pakistan, we have lost tens of thousands as a consequence.

In the years since 9/11 and the US invasion of Afghanistan, Pakistan has become a much more violent society. And I am not referring just to drone attacks by US military agencies that are supposedly aimed at specific or alleged terrorists but end up killing dozens of innocent people, including children, in remote rural locations, spawning disaffection and anti-Americanism. That aside, our domestic structure has been wrecked. Guns and bombs have become much easier to find in Pakistan. In many senses, terrorism and the so-called war on terror have become an industry. Political scores are being settled and private fortunes being built under the cover of fighting the Taliban or Al Qaeda. Organized crime and vendetta politics are being indulged in and conveniently being blamed on terrorist groups that may or may not be responsible. I know this for a fact because I have suffered personally, especially in the case of the attack on the Marriott in Islamabad in 2008. The only people who have benefited after 9/11 are the generals and politicians who have made deals with the US. They have become obscenely rich. A friend once asked me why I was upset: 'Surely your hotels must be full of officials and media persons after 9/11?' I lost my temper. 'Our hotels,' I said, 'are intended to showcase Pakistani hospitality and to welcome tourists who will add to the local economy and help ordinary Pakistanis. I haven't built these hotels because I want people to come and get a ringside view of a war and to mock my country as a basket-case.' None of this would have happened if Musharraf had not so easily thrown up his hands and agreed to obey US orders in September 2001. I still cannot forgive him for that thoughtless decision.

Musharraf let Pakistan down in other areas too. Yes, he was ambitious and well-spoken, he had an educated and modern mind, he was far removed from religious zealots. However, he did little to push reforms in Pakistani society, particularly in terms of the influence of religious laws on daily life—a poisonous legacy of the Zia years—or to revamp our education system. He wasted opportunities and went back on promises. His entire focus was on externalities, on projecting a good image, on symbols and not substance, and on trying to impress Western interlocutors—whether politicians or diplomats, generals or journalists. Take the economy. He made no sizeable public investments in infrastructure like dams or power projects or, for that matter, in universities or technical education institutions. If there is a power crisis in Pakistan or if its educational facilities cannot keep pace with the growing youth population, it is because enlightened decisions were not taken during Musharraf's decade in power. He did not bother about anticipating the needs of the coming years, or about worrying that 40 per cent of Pakistan's population was under the age of twenty and would require classrooms and jobs, not bullets and bluster. Musharraf was lucky in that the Pakistani farmer laboured hard and produced bumper crops in the first decade of the twenty-first century. Cotton, rice, wheat and sugar production went up appreciably. This had nothing to do with the government but was the result of the ordinary tiller's tireless labour in the hot sun, in parched faraway fields.

After 9/11, as Pakistan again became an ally of the US and Europe, the sanctions imposed after the 1998 nuclear tests were eased and Pakistan was given market access for key agricultural and (cotton) textile exports. The benefits of this did not percolate down to the farmer but were grabbed by well-connected intermediaries, some of them close to the generals who ran Islamabad. Pakistan's foreign exchange reserves soared because of these exports, as did government revenues. Rather than reinvest this in the real economy, in infrastructure and job creation, Musharraf frittered it away. He erred grievously in appointing Shaukat Aziz his finance minister and later PM. Shaukat Aziz had spent many years in Citibank, using his connections in the Gulf countries to encourage rich Arabs to invest in Citibank's portfolio schemes. Shaukat Aziz was a devotee of the capital markets, not of brick-and-mortar businesses and genuine economic growth and development. He forced government corporations to put their surpluses in the stock exchange. When the markets crashed in 2007/08, millions of dollars were lost. This was not private money. It belonged to the people of Pakistan. Finally, in 2007, Musharraf was persuaded to promulgate the National Reconciliation Ordinance, a controversial law that granted amnesty to all those (including politicians, public servants and businessmen) accused of corruption, bribery and money laundering between 1986 and 1999. I was horrified. Millions of dollars of bad loans were written off. As a businessman who had always repaid his loans and never defaulted, I felt this was daylight robbery. It betrayed public trust and legitimized the theft of public money. Extremely unscrupulous but well-connected people had been let off with the stroke of a pen.

The National Reconciliation Ordinance was part of a deal between Musharraf and Benazir, who was negotiating her return to Pakistan. Ironically, the biggest beneficiaries of Musharraf's ordinance were Zardari and other leading lights of the PPP. Yet again, a self-serving elite had failed Pakistan.

In 2002, Musharraf held a referendum that extended his term as President by five years. In the intervening period, he started believing that he was a popular, charismatic leader and could rule for much longer. His problems were exacerbated in 2007 when he took on the Supreme Court and sought to sack Chief Justice Iftikhar Chaudhary and fourteen other judges. For a man who claimed to uphold Pakistan's institutions, Musharraf set out to destroy the independence of the Supreme Court because Justice Chaudhary had started to ask tough questions. Thirty-five jurists and many lawyers were placed under house arrest. Mass protests broke out. The judiciary's determined resistance caused the dam of public impatience to burst. Musharraf found the ground beneath his feet slipping.

In 2007, I came out in support of Justice Chaudhary. I didn't know him personally but was disheartened at the manner in which a resolute judge was being hounded by the military junta. The legal community appreciated my efforts. In his presidential message in the Supreme Court Bar Association of Pakistan, *Directory 2008*, the well-known Pakistani lawyer and public intellectual Aitzaz Ahsan made special mention of my 'warm cooperation' to the struggle of the legal community.

Musharraf lost a lot of goodwill by trying to scuttle the judiciary. The straight-shooting general of 1999 had become just another politician by 2007. It was unfortunate. For some years after that, Musharraf lived in Dubai. We met occasionally but rarely discussed politics. He had gone through a lot, as a general and as a politician, and I respected that. He was pleasant and engaging. Even so, his advisers kept urging him to set up a political party. All I could tell him was, 'Don't do it. Be happy with what you achieved over eight years.' But he continued to surround himself with those who told him what he wanted to hear, and began to live under the delusion that vast sections of people in Pakistan were waiting to welcome him back. When he decided to return, I counselled him not to. He was adamant. 'You should see the following I have on Twitter and Facebook,' he told me. I shrugged my shoulders and could only say, 'Thank God I don't have a Facebook account!'

The other epochal event in Pakistan towards the end of 2007 was the return of Benazir Bhutto. As elections approached in early 2008, Benazir came home after nine years of exile in Dubai and London. Landing in Karachi on 18 October 2007, she was greeted not only by huge crowds but also by a bomb attack as she was travelling from the airport. While she escaped without any harm, over 100 people were killed. This was testimony to how politics and life in Pakistan had changed since the conflict was reignited in Afghanistan. I couldn't meet Benazir but kept track of her arrival and reception by her supporters. I heard news from various sources that she was being targeted by assassins and, in fact, sent her a message of warning. I didn't know it then but the person through whom I sent the letter, a senior PPP politician, was later himself suspected to be part of the conspiracy. On 27 December, Benazir was killed while leaving an election meeting in Rawalpindi's Liaquat Bagh. As she stood up and emerged from the sunroof of her vehicle, she was shot at. Within seconds, explosives were detonated near the vehicle. Various groups—Al Qaeda, Taliban, Lashkar-e-Jhangvi, and so on—were blamed for the assassination but I always believed that it was a political plot. Within two hours of her killing, Sindh was on fire. Banks were robbed, ATMs were ransacked. Safes and lockers in banks were forcibly opened with fairly sophisticated tools that cannot ʾe easily collected. It was so well planned, as if someone had turned on a switch. Benazir had many faults but the fact was that she cared for Pakistan dearly. Before taking that flight to Karachi, she had built her alliances with the US and the World Bank. Had she won the 2008 election, as was widely expected, she may have had the political capital and resources to embark on a mission of economic reconstruction. Common friends who spoke to her in 2007 say she admitted to her mistakes of the early 1990s and had evolved since. Perhaps this was true, perhaps not—we will never know. What Benazir would have been like in her third term as PM will remain one of the perennial what-ifs of Pakistani history. What we do know is that too many people in the government, the political establishment, and the PPP itself wanted Benazir out of the way. Those who gained from her death could have formed a coalition to abruptly remove her from public life.

After all, somebody stood to benefit from her blood.

11

IN THE RING OF FIRE

Benazir's assassination was a cathartic moment for many Pakistanis of my generation. It didn't matter if you were a PPP supporter and old Bhutto loyalist, or if you had opposed them through the years. That was not the issue, not at this sombre hour. What Benazir's passing indicated, and indicated rudely, was that the old ways and old days had gone forever. The Bhutto family, which had had such a grip on public life in Pakistan since the early 1970s and was blessed with the mesmerizing oratory of Zulfikar Ali Bhutto, would never again have the larger-than-life presence that it once did, not even if Benazir's young son stayed on in politics. There was acute realization that Pakistan as a society had been transformed for perhaps all time to come or, at least, for the foreseeable future. It was a wake-up call for those who believed the violence and internal bloodletting that had risen dramatically and exponentially in the period following 9/11 and the new war in Afghanistan were temporary phenomena. They now realized this was not just a bad dream that would end soon. It had altered something fundamental. A new and sinister type of political activism had taken root in Pakistan. It spoke not with words but with bullets and bombs.

Pakistan had seen violent phases earlier. The politics of Karachi was often enmeshed with organized crime and extortion, as I have described earlier (*see* chapter 10) but all that seemed petty compared to what we were experiencing now. A multitude of terrorist groups and religious-extremist private armies, all of them intersecting with crime syndicates backed by senior politicians; a culture of suicide bombings; attacks on foreigners, whether Chinese engineers working on a project or Sri Lankan cricketers (Lahore, March 2009); the brutal assassination of a mainstream politician and former PM within weeks of her return from years in exile—a tectonic shift had occurred in our country.

Benazir's death also ended the effective political career of Pervez Musharraf. It hurt his credibility and laid bare the insecurity and lawlessness that had become the norm in Pakistan. In October 2007, Musharraf had got the outgoing

National Assembly to re-elect him President. He had formally resigned from the army and now fancied himself as a civilian President, boasting that he would be the head of state for another five-year term. This was part of an arrangement he had worked out with his Western patrons and with Benazir. It would allow him to be a stakeholder in the power matrix in Islamabad, while giving Benazir a likely shot at the prime ministership. General elections were scheduled for 8 January 2008, and it was predicted Benazir's party would emerge with a majority. A concert of power involving Musharraf as President and Benazir as PM was what the Western powers seemed to be working towards. Interfering blatantly in Pakistani politics, they were trying to isolate Nawaz Sharif, even though he was the most popular politician in Punjab. This neat plan fell to pieces after Benazir's death. The election to the National Assembly was postponed to February 2008 and resulted in an inconclusive verdict. The PPP, benefiting from the sympathy following Benazir's murder, finished as the single largest party but won little over 30 per cent of the seats. The PML (N) came second, with about a quarter of the seats. It was a horribly hung legislature. Eventually, the two biggest parties and their leaders—Zardari and Nawaz Sharif—had to agree to form a government for national unity and come together in a coalition. It was also obvious they would have to choose a new President, as impeachment proceedings against Musharraf began fairly soon. Nawaz Sharif's party had not forgiven him for the coup of 1999 and wanted him punished. The vitriolic and oppressive campaign Musharraf had undertaken against the judiciary had hurt him and left him with few friends in Islamabad. Finally, the assassination of Benazir, and the violence that both preceded and followed it, exposed Musharraf's claims of having rescued Pakistan from disaster. His folly in aligning himself with distant powers—and their high-risk games and endless military adventures in Afghanistan—was now apparent to all. It had made Pakistan a precarious society and a much more dangerous place. In contrast, the 1990s seemed almost idyllic (though they were far from it). His legacy in tatters, Musharraf was forced to resign in August 2008. Three months later, he left the country and flew to London and then Dubai.

After the general election, Yousaf Raza Gillani, a veteran of the PPP, became PM. Real power, however, was moving to Zardari. When Benazir had returned to Pakistan in 2007, she had been told by well-wishers that her husband's reputation had damaged her earlier stints as PM. She had indicated she understood this and had told Zardari he would have to live abroad and keep away from the country and the PPP in case she formed a government again. That was an informal condition she had placed. Now Benazir was dead. Her brother and challenger to the political inheritance of the Bhutto family, Murtaza, had been killed by the police years earlier. Benazir's son, Bilawal, was too young to seek public office. This left Zardari, a political carpetbagger if ever there was one, as the custodian of the PPP. With Musharraf's stars on the decline and with the West unwilling to place full trust in Nawaz Sharif—partly because of lobbying by Zardari and his agents and proxies in Washington DC and London— the power dynamic changed. Zardari manoeuvred himself into the good books of the big powers—which had substantial leverage in Pakistan after September 2001— and became the most powerful politician in the country. To those who had known him in his early years, this was absolutely unbelievable. In September 2008, Zardari stood for indirect elections to the presidency. Candidates were required to be college graduates, and Zardari was not one. In his nomination forms, he said he had got a business degree from an institution in London. Tellingly, no degree or certificate was ever produced. Those of us familiar with his background couldn't recall any such degree or certificate.

I met Zardari shortly after he became President. His body language and the glint in his eyes were disturbing. Later that evening, a British journalist whom I had known for some years and who was visiting Pakistan came to see me. 'What do you think of your new President?' he asked.

I kept quiet, holding back my thoughts. The journalist repeated the question: 'What do you think of your new President?' I had to reply. 'Not much,' I said, softly. 'Well,' my visitor said, 'for a man whose country is in crisis and who's lost his wife in an awful tragedy only a few months ago, he certainly seems to smile a lot.' I didn't say anything, but the message was conveyed. A lot of people who met Zardari in that period came away with a similar perception. As President, Zardari was supremely lucky. The army did not want to interfere directly in politics. After the Musharraf experience, it felt it had to give—and had to be seen to be giving—democratic politics a fair chance. Further, Zardari won over key generals by giving them job extensions. Influential sections in the West had come to an understanding with Zardari and were keen to give Pakistan a civilian face so that they could pretend they had ended military rule and were encouraging democracy.

The Enhanced Partnership with Pakistan Act (2009)—also called the Kerry–Lugar Act, named for Senators John Kerry and Richard Lugar—was a US legislation designed to provide financial support to Zardari's regime and weaken the army by shackling it. The military was on the defensive. Gillani and the other ministers were in any case handicapped by the fact that they were part of a weak and fragmented government. Zardari took advantage of all this. As PPP head, he ensured he had no in-house dissidents. Gradually, he converted the party into a fiefdom. Old-school politicians from his father-in-law's time, many of whom had been around in the 1990s to guide Benazir, were marginalized by Zardari. This left Zardari with absolute power. A man who had not won a popular election, and probably never would, was presiding over the destiny of 200 million people. As could be expected, he was back to his old tricks very soon. Only this time, he had an alibi—all disturbances could be blamed on that omnibus word: 'terrorism'. In reality, the presidency was run like a cartel. In his motivations and methods, the Zardari of 2008 was no different from the Zardari of 1990. If anything, he was worse—Mr Ten Per Cent had become Mr Ninety Per Cent.

It was not a coincidence that I began to feel like a hunted man. A sense of déjà vu overcame me; it was 1990 once again though, this time, the stakes were higher. In 2008 and 2009, there were five attempts on my life. My house in Islamabad was set on fire. An act of arson led to a blaze in the headquarters of the Hashoo Group in the United Bank Tower in Islamabad, in the very office rooms where I went to work every day. In June 2009, the Pearl Continental Peshawar was the subject of a vicious bomb attack. Seventeen people were killed, including a very senior UN official. The most audacious assault on the Hashoo Group took place, of course, on 20 September

2008. It was a day of infamy, a day I will never forget. I was in Islamabad that evening and praying when the ground shook under me. Almost simultaneously, my phone rang. I ignored the phone and continued praying. It was 8.03 p.m. when I took the call. What I was told shocked me. It was an executive from the Marriott Hotel. Nine minutes earlier, at 7.54 p.m., a suicide bomber had driven a large, explosive-laden truck up to the hotel and blown himself up. I shivered. On a normal day, I would have been in the hotel already; in fact, I was expected for dinner to celebrate the birthday of Sumeira, the wife of my son Murtaza. I was driving to the hotel from another family occasion, the birthday party of my grandson Ali, my daughter Nadia's son. (Ali was born on 16 September but the party had been held four days later that year.) Before I got to the hotel, I decided to stop by at the mosque for prayers. That saved me from death. As I left the mosque, a sense of dread enveloped me. A hundred thoughts swirled in my mind and I prayed to the Almighty as I ran to the car and rushed to the hotel. I reached to see not the beautiful hotel that we had so lovingly built, but a war zone. There had been 2000 people in the hotel when the bombing happened. Sixty people had died, close to 300 people were injured. We found bodies of our dear guests, colleagues, friends: faces I recognized, faces I had worked with and smiled at. The sight that stunned me was the crater—

60 feet wide and 20 feet deep. It had been created by over 1000 kg of RDX. The hotel had not been attacked—it had been brutalized. Dead bodies and dismembered limbs, pools of blood—it was a massacre. I had thought of myself as a hardened man who had seen violence and grisly sights—but what I saw that day will be engraved in my memory for the rest of my life.

As soon as I reached, local and international journalists wanted to speak to me. I was too emotionally spent to talk at length but I remember one of my first sentences: 'I'm not concerned about this hotel. We can rebuild it, but who is going to bring back the people who have been killed?'

The Islamabad Marriott Hotel is located on Aga Khan Road. This is in a very high-security zone, the Islamabad equivalent of the Washington DC Beltway. The Parliament and the Supreme Court, the President's residence, and the PM's workplace as well as home—all of these are located close by. It is not an area where you can simply drive around for the sake of it. Cars from outside the zone, not owned by the government or without the requisite security clearances, are not usually seen on the roads near the Marriott. It struck me as odd that a whole truck, packed with explosives and undetected by security officials and policemen who regularly patrolled the area, had not just entered this high-security zone but done so without being stopped. At 7.54 p.m., the eight-wheeled dumper truck, apparently escorted by a car—took a sharp turn towards the main entrance of the Marriott. The pilot car veered off in another direction and drove off, its job done. The truck driver found his path blocked by the massive steel barrier at the hotel entrance. The barrier is hydraulically operated and lowered only when any waiting car has been checked by our security team. The truck struck the barrier but couldn't break it. This happened at very high speed, and the truck's large fender got entangled in a part of the steel barrier. Right then, one of the truck's tyres burst. Hotel security officials rushed towards the truck to stop the driver from causing further damage. In those precious seconds, the driver detonated some explosives and the truck burst into flames.

Immediately, our security team deployed fire extinguishers but the flames were too much for the extinguishers. The attack was only a diversion. Four minutes later, the driver activated the bulk of the explosives in the truck. The explosion was massive and earth-shattering. The hotel building bore the brunt of the shockwaves. This was the suicide attack. The driver-assailant died immediately but 1000 kg of explosives did their worst against the Marriott and those inside. Two minutes later, something strange happened. Fires broke out in rooms on the fourth and fifth floors of the hotel building. Those who saw the fires presumed that this was a consequence of the truck explosion and that flames were spreading rapidly and vertically upwards. However, the flames in the rooms on the fourth and fifth floors were blue in colour. Explosive and forensic specialists said that blue flames indicated fresh fires caused by chemicals. They could not have been the result of ordinary fires spreading in a building and causing, say, curtains and bed linen or tables and chairs to burn. This was confirmed by investigators who visited those rooms and concluded that temperatures inside had reached 300°C. Obviously, independent fires had been triggered in those rooms, using chemicals that were different and separate from the RDX in the truck.

To be honest, all of this didn't strike me right then. I was bewildered and busy with the rescue effort. I was mortified at the senseless killing of innocent people, ordinary men and women who had placed their trust in our hotel and come to stay or dine there—and humble Pakistanis who worked with pride in their capital's best-known hotel. Gritting my teeth, I exclaimed at one point, 'You bastards have done what you have to. Now I'll do what I have to. We'll rebuild this hotel and have it up and running in three months—ninety days.' I don't know from where I found the words to set that deadline. At the time, I didn't even know the extent of the damage. It was an impulsive and spontaneous promise. I felt I owed it to all those who had died and suffered on that black day. Meanwhile, my daughter Sarah and the peerless members of the hotel staff were spearheading the rescue effort. Medicos from hospitals and, of course, the police had also arrived. 'Why have I been targeted?' I kept asking myself. Was there a pattern on all these attacks on me? Given the Marriott's location and the number of international guests it had, it was likely that this was a high-profile terror strike by some crazy extremist group.

I began to have second thoughts when two Pakistani journalists walked up to me and asked questions. 'Mr Hashwani,' the first of the two men began, 'I understand President Zardari was the target of the bombing. What do you have to say about it?' 'Really?' I said. 'But he was not supposed to be at our hotel. There was no event planned here. I would have known if the President was coming. I think you're mistaken.' The journalist looked surprised. His friend picked up the conversation, 'Are you sure?' 'Of course I'm sure, my friend,' I said, putting my hand on his shoulder, 'now if you'll excuse me . . .' With that I went off to help a colleague who was trying to assist an injured person. I would have thought nothing of it and dismissed it as a journalist verifying hearsay and rumour if, shortly afterwards, I had not received a telephone call from a senior government official. Without much ado, without commiserating or asking how serious the situation was, without a word of condolence for the human casualties, he came straight to his message: 'You must tell the media that the President was intended to be the target of the bombing.' 'But how can I?' I replied. 'He was not even booked to come here. Why should I lie? I'm not going to lie on behalf of him or anybody . . .'

Nevertheless, Zardari and his office began to tell the international media that he was scheduled to have dinner at the Marriott with some parliamentarians and the bombing had been planned to kill him. The dinner had been cancelled at the last moment, he claimed. When journalists came to me, I denied it again. There were no bookings for any dinner and no cancellations; I'd checked and rechecked with the GM. What was Zardari doing? Ever one for publicity, he was presenting himself as a warrior against and victim of terrorism, one who had lost his wife and was now in danger himself. This was a great story to spread just before a visit to the US. When he reached Washington DC a few days later, he told CNN in an interview that he had been the target of the bombing, that he was high on the alleged hit list of terror groups, and that he was the world's frontline soldier in the 'war against terror'. Right after the interview, CNN played a clipping of me confirming that the attack had not been aimed at the President and there had been no dinner event that evening that he was ever supposed to have attended. This punctured the story somewhat, but when had something as inconvenient as fact ever stopped Zardari?

In the days that followed, I was at the Marriott site every day, personally supervising debris removal and reconstruction. I had to rebuild the hotel in ninety days; I owed that to the memory of those who had been martyred on 20 September 2008. I went to countless funerals and visited the families and homes of as many people as I could. It was wrenching to meet the parents or families of colleagues with whom we had spent happy times, but who were now gone forever. Meeting little children who had been orphaned was extremely difficult. What can you tell a little child who said goodbye to a loving father in the morning, fully expecting to see him in the evening? How can you console such a child? What can you say to her? What explanations will suffice? I buried myself in work and channelled my emotions into the mission to rebuild the Marriott. It became my constant companion. There were days when I spent eighteen to twenty hours at the site, coming home too exhausted to do anything but sleep. 'It's the only way I can stay sane,' I told a friend.

In all this, I was also carefully monitoring the investigation. I wanted justice for those who had died in the hotel. I wanted the culprits and masterminds punished. However, several pieces did not seem to fit. First, there was the discrepancy between the truck's explosives and the chemical fires on the fourth and fifth floors. Then there was the mystery of how the truck had been allowed to travel through a high-security zone without anybody stopping it. It had entered a neighbourhood where the PM was hosting an iftar evening for 400 people. The President, several members of the cabinet, senior officials from the civil service and the army, and leading diplomats were at this iftar. It was held at the PM's house, barely a kilometre from the Marriott. Incredibly, a truck filled with explosives had driven past! What of the car that had guided the truck to the Marriott? It was as if it had navigated the route and directed the driver—presumably an outsider, unfamiliar with the geography of inner Islamabad—to the hotel. Closed-circuit TV cameras had captured the registration number of the car, just as it went off in another direction, allowing the truck to drive towards the entrance of the Marriott. Despite these pictures, the car was never traced. All one could hear in the aftermath of the attack was that the President had been targeted. That was the only propaganda coming from the government.

It was clear to me and to most in the security establishment that Zardari was not even remotely the target of the Marriott bombing. That was the story that had been spun for the Western media. So who was the target? Was it an attack on the most conspicuous Islamabad location where, at any given time, politicians, government officials, leading businessmen, and foreign dignitaries could be expected to stay or dine? Was it just a coincidence that the

Hashoo Group owned the hotel? On the other hand, was I the target? How did one explain the fires in my United Bank Tower offices and at my residence in Islamabad—and the threat to my life? While the Marriott was being rebuilt, there were at least three attempts on my life. On two occasions, gangs of strange men, carrying weapons, walked into the hotel reconstruction site just like that. On both occasions, I had been warned in advance by police officials, and escaped. The events left me tossing and turning at night. Was someone sending me a message? I spoke to a friend in intelligence. He heard me out, and promised to get back after some snooping. A few days later, he came to see me and said, 'Mr Hashwani, you are the target. And it's not the Taliban or any of those fellows who are after you . . . There's a political conspiracy I think . . . But I don't want to say more. Be careful. That's all I can say.'

After the officer left, I thought long and hard about what he had said. He seemed to confirm my assessment—and this was not limited to the strike on the Marriott or the other attacks on me or facilities linked with me—that the so-called 'war against terror' and the depredations of the Taliban and other Islamist groups had become a convenient cover for the conduct of organized criminal operations and political vendetta. Opponents were being eliminated or frightened, perhaps forced to run away or sell assets cheap. Was this happening to me as well? How could I explain the spurt in attacks on me? After so many years, why were the Taliban and Al Qaeda and their affiliate groups suddenly so keen to get rid of Sadruddin Hashwani? What was the reason—or was this just the story that was being spread? On the day the Marriott was attacked, I got a telephone call from Rehman Malik, then the interior minister and an acolyte of Zardari's. He was sympathetic and asked me over. When I reached his residence, he was kind enough to offer me dinner. It was 1 a.m. Five hours had passed since the terror strike. I was drained and tired beyond belief. 'I don't want dinner,' I said. 'A cup of tea would be welcome though . . .' As the tea arrived, I asked aloud—addressing Rehman Malik, you could say, or no one in particular—'Who did this?' Pat came the answer: 'Obviously Baitullah Mehsud.' I was surprised. Baitullah Mehsud was an extremist leader from the Waziristan region who had emerged as a commander of the 'Pakistan Taliban'. How did the minister know so quickly, within five hours, that Mehsud was responsible for the destruction of my hotel? Just what was going on? I stared at him, and my mind raced. Could I ignore the signs? Could I ignore that the threat perception to me had risen enormously in recent months? Could I brush aside the kidnapping threats that my son Murtaza had received even before the Marriott bombing? Was this a throwback to the days of Bashir Qureshi and the Karachi of the early 1990s (*see* chapter 9) but played out on a larger canvas? Had Pakistan, my beloved Pakistan, become too risky for me? In 1990, I had had to relocate to London for three months—would I have to do something similar now? I was conscious that it was not just me but my entire family that had escaped narrowly. On 20 September 2008, when the truck hit the hotel barrier, my son Murtaza was approaching the Marriott. Hearing the sound, he panicked, since he presumed I was already in the hotel. As he accelerated, a police officer refused to let him proceed, telling him there had been an accident with a truck. Murtaza argued but the policeman did not listen and forced him to turn his car from the very edge of the Marriott. Murtaza drove off, still uncertain where I was, as I was not answering my mobile phone. Then, right then, the suicide bomber detonated the RDX. From his car, Murtaza saw the horror. The policeman who had urged him to get away died in the explosion. His action had saved Murtaza's life. Allah had saved Murtaza, and saved us, but the enemy had put us on notice.

In the interim, the Marriott reconstruction continued at a frenetic pace. I was determined to meet the ninety-day deadline and reopen the hotel on 20 December 2008. My mind was full of questions. Should I go overseas for some time? Would that seem like running away after an attack of this nature? What signal would it send to my business associates and colleagues in Pakistan? Going to the West was not an option—it was too far away and would seem like seeking shelter in the same countries that had played such havoc with Pakistan and its periphery. I decided to leave for Dubai till the heat died down and till the threat to my life receded. It was close enough to Karachi and Islamabad for me to make trips back home—I expected to be away for only a few months—and was a welcoming, safe and well-equipped city. Dubai would allow me to not just run my affairs in Pakistan from a short distance but also make it convenient to do business in other parts of Asia and Africa, all of which had convenient air connections from Dubai. I shared my plans with my family and a few trusted confidants. We planned to leave after the reopening of the hotel on 20 December.

Unfortunately, we couldn't keep to the ninety-day deadline that I had promised to myself and the world. We missed it by eight days. The Marriott opened its doors to guests on 28 December 2008, ninety-eight days after the attack. The ceremony was attended by leading residents of Islamabad, including the ambassadors of the US and Saudi Arabia. Against the advice of security agencies, I drove the same evening to Lahore to attend the wedding of the Pearl Continental's GM's daughter. Immediately after that, I flew to Dubai. It was one year and one day since Benazir had been killed. What a nightmare of a year it had been. As I watched Lahore's gleaming lights from the plane, I had tears in my eyes and resolved to be back soon. How was I to know that it would be five years before I saw my beloved country again?

From Dubai, I oversaw my business. It was disheartening, on the other hand, to see my country crumble. The Zardari years saw an institutionalizing of crime and corruption. In earlier days, the army would have intervened and offered a corrective. In the period after 2008, it was forced to sit on the margins because the US was desperate to pretend that it was using 'democratic' leaders in Pakistan to fight 'terrorism'. Zardari and his acolytes did all that Musharraf was accused of and more. There was lawlessness in large swathes of Pakistan, particularly Balochistan and Sindh. Extortion and kidnapping for ransom were rampant. Supreme Court judgements were violated and public money funnelled away. It was a free-for-all and caused many to flee the country or move money and investments abroad. Some of the flight of capital could also be explained by PPP functionaries and ministers parking their embezzled wealth abroad.

In 2010 in Dubai, I met a former US diplomat, now working for a think tank in Washington DC. He was on his way back from Pakistan. 'Tell me, Mr Hashwani,' he asked, 'why are so many people I know in Pakistan investing or opening bank accounts abroad, in Dubai or London or Singapore? Why are they sending their children out of the country?' 'Please ask our President,' I said, without batting an eyelid. 'You placed him there to save our country. Won't you ask if he's succeeding?' The visitor smiled sardonically. Every week, every day would bring disturbing news from Pakistan. In January 2011, I heard about the shocking assassination of Salman Taseer, an old friend and then the Governor of Punjab. He was gunned down by his bodyguard—shot by the man assigned to protect him. I was distraught, for Salman had been an associate for decades, a man full of life, from a family we knew very well. In the late 1960s and early 1970s, on his return from London after qualifying as a chartered accountant, Salman had done some work with our companies. Quick-witted and handsome, he had a larger-than-life personality. I used to meet him socially in Islamabad as well and it was hard to accept that he was gone. We were very different as individuals. He liked his drink and was fond of the high life—those are not my interests but someone else's personal life does not bother me. Unfortunately, the personal and the public cannot be easily demarcated when you take political office—as Salman had—especially in the new Pakistan. A few days before he was killed, Salman was in Dubai and came over to my office, then in Emirates Towers, for lunch. I ordered Peking duck, for I knew he liked it. We sat down and chatted like the old friends we were. He joked and gossiped and showed me text messages on his mobile phone, messages from his lady friends. Obviously, he was still living a carefree life, even though he had become Governor and was no more a private citizen. This got me a little concerned.

'Tell me, Salman,' I asked, 'do you take your guards with you when you go to meet your girlfriends?' 'Yes, of course,' he said. 'And they see you going in and coming out?' I asked. 'Yes,' he nodded. 'How do you trust them?' I carried on, 'They could misunderstand completely. They have grown up in a different Pakistan, Zia's Pakistan . . . They could be religious extremists!' 'Oh come on, Sadru,' he said, waving his hand, 'I don't care.' A week later, Salman was dead. He was exiting a restaurant in Islamabad when his own guard shot him. The provocation had been that Salman had spoken in favour of a Christian woman who had been sentenced to death under Pakistan's anti-blasphemy laws. Salman could be brash and loose with his language. It was okay among friends and people from a similar background. The bodyguard did not share these sensibilities. In Islamabad's most trendy and coveted shopping district, the guard pumped twenty-six bullets into Salman's body. I didn't sleep well that night. How much more could Pakistan take? How many friends would I lose? How many friends would still be around when I returned to Pakistan? Would

I ever return to Pakistan? Yes, I would, I told myself, I would. One day . . .

~

Postscript: Elections were held in Pakistan in May 2013. The PML (N) won 166 of the 342 seats in the National Assembly, just short of a majority. Nawaz Sharif became PM, helped by the fact that his brother Shahbaz Sharif had done well as Punjab chief minister and helped the provincial economy recover. This was what people had voted for—peace and prosperity, jobs and electricity, low prices and quality education for their children. They were fed up of the Zardari years and of the PPP. More than anything else, they were tired of a war they didn't want or understand or invite upon themselves. On 14 June 2013, I flew back to Pakistan. It was my first journey to my motherland in four and a half years. I was overwhelmed and extremely emotional that day. I had never expected I would be away for so long. Zardari was still President (his term ended in September 2013) but he was a lame duck. The government he ran so ruthlessly was gone and Nawaz Sharif was now the PM.

I reached home and slept on my bed in Islamabad for the first time in years. I sought an audience with the new PM, and he welcomed me and Sarah very warmly. He was supportive and sympathetic. He knew the circumstances of my exile and the background. 'You are a brave man and a fighter,' he said. I told him it was difficult to fight one's government, especially when it was determined to cause harm, but I had gone through it without regret and with the blessings of Allah. I told him of the new hotels I was planning in Pakistan and assured him that my investments in and commitment to Pakistan were sacrosanct. Later, Sarah and I flew to Lahore and met Shahbaz Sharif. In my personal capacity, I had supported the setting up of an art gallery in Lahore. It depicted the philosophy of Allama Iqbal, the poet-intellectual who dreamt of a homeland for British India's Muslims and helped shape the foundational ideology of Pakistan. The paintings with which the gallery started out were by Syed Sadequain Ahmed Naqvi—or simply Sadequain, as he was known. One of the most accomplished artists of Pakistan, Sadequain is a personal favourite of mine. He died in 1987. The gallery, inaugurated by Shahbaz Sharif on 24 June 2013, is a tribute to both Sadequain and, of course, the great Iqbal.

Nawaz Sharif has a huge challenge ahead of him. In end-2014, the US troops will leave Afghanistan and that will create a security vacuum, the contours of which are impossible to predict. That apart, the economic crisis in Pakistan needs to be addressed. The previous government left the country reeling under a mountain of debt.

Infrastructure was creaking, power cuts were rampant, food prices were high, and job creation was non-existent. Nawaz Sharif had inherited a perfect storm. His principal mandate was to nurse the wounds of Pakistan and repair the damage done in the final years of Musharraf and the five years of Zardari and his party. I wished him well and still pray for him each morning. For Pakistan's sake, he has to succeed.

12

NEW FRONTIERS, OLD DREAMS

When I was a young boy, a favourite uncle told me, 'Sadru, you have a warrior in you.' This was a jesting, teasing remark about my stubbornness. Looking back at my childhood, I can find nothing but appreciation for my remarkable parents. I was a difficult boy to bring up, always insistent on doing things my way, and they showed generous patience and tolerance. The independent streak that so amused my uncle all those years ago has stayed with me through life. Has it served me well or poorly? I leave that to you, who have come so far with me and read the preceding chapters of this book, to decide. The fact is that without the stubbornness and the free-spiritedness I would not be who I am. I have been a fighter through my adult life and my career. I have fought what I considered injustice and unfair regulation and inequitable administration. I have fought petty bureaucrats and I have fought megalomaniacal presidents. To borrow the words of that famed Frank Sinatra song, 'I've done it my way'. An old friend, who has known me for many, many years, visited me while I was in the midst of yet another one of my innumerable battles against the Pakistani government. We were sitting in a group and some of the others—well-meaning people who had my best interests at heart—nudged me towards compromising with the authorities. 'Go and meet the PM,' one of them said, 'you know that's all that is needed. It can be sorted out.' I refused, 'No way!' My friend had been watching this exchange silently. Finally, he spoke, and did so with a smile on his face. 'When faced with a choice,' he said, 'Sadru will always take the most difficult option.' At this, everybody broke into a laugh and even I couldn't resist a big smile. What my friend had said was true. The line of least resistance is not for me—the long and straight path is what I instinctively prefer.

Having said that, let me not pretend that life has been only a battleground. On the contrary, it has been very rewarding. The munificence that Allah has showered upon me has given me more than I deserved or dreamt of. Here I am not referring to just material wealth, for that is ephemeral; you will leave it all behind when you leave the Earth, your palms empty. My reference is to the richness of experiences and the love of so many people, colleagues and friends, and my loving children and now grandchildren. Allah has allowed me to fulfil my fantasies and dreams, to indulge myself in the best possible manner. When I was a boy, my father used to take me to the port side in Karachi. We would spend the evening there, with my father pointing out the big ships and the lights in the distance. My father was passionate about ships, as I wrote earlier. Even without meaning to, he transmitted this passion to me. There we would stand, father and son, wide-eyed, staring at the ships, and wondering where they were going and where they were coming from, lost in our thoughts, lost to the world. Consider the greatness of the Almighty. When I grew up, that very port and those very ships—or at least ships just like those—became central to my life. I spent so many meaningful days and weeks and months and years amid those massive seafaring vessels. I lived my dream.

I have always been a proud, patriotic Pakistani. I grew up in the early years of Independence, in the 1950s, when the idealism of our founders was with us. We were a more innocent and accepting society then, and had a rose-tinted vision for Pakistan and all Pakistanis. The differences and the sectarianism and parochialism of later decades did not exist then, at least not to any critical degree. As a child, I read and followed all I could about the diversity and the various regions of Pakistan. Though I lived in Karachi and hardly got to see even rural Sindh—the province of which Karachi is the capital—it was my desire and wish to see the rest of Pakistan, so that the names and places marked in my geography book or on the map of my country could come alive to me. Here too, fate was kind to me. I have travelled up and down Pakistan, seen it closely as few others have. I have been fortunate to experience the range that Pakistan offers—from humble fishing villages in remote areas of Balochistan to the soirées of the high and mighty in Islamabad. Twice, in the 1980s under Zia and in the mid-1990s, during Nawaz Sharif's second term, I went underground to escape arrest on false charges. During these periods, I travelled through rural Punjab, to the tribal areas and the Frontier territories of Khyber Pakhtunkhwa. I spent nights in small villages, among very ordinary but amazingly hospitable Pakistanis. This gave me a window to our society that I would otherwise never have got. Despite the troubles I underwent and notwithstanding the dangers I faced from oppressive governments, those voyages into the vastness of Pakistan did not just satisfy my curiosity and sense of inquiry, but also made me love and cherish Pakistan that much more.

The Hashoo Group is well known for its hotel chain but, for me, the hotels have never been work—rather, they have been an obsessive hobby. I have always been fascinated with hotels—on the surface, the luxury and splendour, but, more substantially, the complexity that goes into the simplicity of prompt and responsive service to the guest. These were aspects that engrossed me well before I owned my first hotel, well before I began working at all. As a young boy, I used to look at pictures of hotels and read about their interiors—their cavernous kitchens, the different types of rooms, the other facilities, and so on. Today, running a hotel or building a hotel from scratch, seeing it emerge from nothingness into a splendid artefact—as in the case of the Pearl Continental Bhurban, for instance—takes me back to those childhood moments. Yet again, I am walking through my dreams.

It takes luck and pluck to convert adversity into opportunity. I moved to Dubai in December 2008 to avoid threats to my life in Pakistan. I thought I would be gone for only a few months; it turned out to be for almost five years. Today, I divide my time between Dubai and Pakistan. The reason I have not moved back full-time to Pakistan is because I have learnt to appreciate the merits of Dubai as an international business metropolis, one that will help me—and the Hashoo Group—explore new frontiers, geographically and otherwise. In the immediate future, while looking to expand our hotel chain in Pakistan, I am focusing on the energy sector—on oil and gas exploration and production. This is the most international of all businesses the Hashoo Group has entered. While we began our oil operations in Pakistan, today we are scouring the world for oil, black gold as it is called: Indonesia to Iraq, Vietnam to Sudan, Kazakhstan to the Philippines, and North Africa to the Gulf of Mexico. Of course, what we are keenest on is the opening up and deregulation of the oil and gas exploration industry in Pakistan itself. Our country is blessed with energy resources, which need to be harnessed to (literally) light up the lives of ordinary people. How did I get interested in the oil business? Here again I need to tell you a story from my early years.

As a young boy, I loved watching films. In 1956, I saw *Giant* at Capitol Cinema in Karachi's Sadar area. Starring Rock Hudson, Elizabeth Taylor and James Dean—it was Dean's last film: he died in a car accident before the film was released—*Giant* was a Hollywood epic and is recognized as an iconic movie. It captures the evolution of a Texan community, from the settled life of agriculture and ranches, to the discovery of oil and the new money this throws up. It also captures the social transformation of a society, the chipping away at racial prejudices and so on. The film left a deep impression on me. The one scene that had me absolutely mesmerized was that of oil gushing rom the ground and James Dean watching in unbelievable delight, completely enthralled. It was the first time I had seen oil emerge from the earth, and with a force and energy that was infectious. It sowed seeds in my mind. One day, I wanted to see this for myself, for real. One day, I wanted to be a part of this world. My little mind was agog with wonder and possibility.

As I grew older, I moved into several lines of business, unrelated to oil and gas. My fascination with the petroleum industry didn't wane though. On business visits to West Asia and the Arab homelands of crude oil, I made it a point to visit exploration and production facilities. You could have called me a petroleum tourist! When I went to the US, my eye was not on New York or San Francisco but on Houston, home to the oil industry and part of Texas, the state in which *Giant* was set and shot. Gradually, my dreams began to enter the workplace. In 1977, I started mining barite in Balochistan. Barite is a mineral used as a drilling fluid in oil and gas exploration. Unfortunately, our barite factory did not do well and had to be shut down. Low volumes made operations unviable. Soon I was importing barite and mud chemicals (or drilling fluid chemicals) for supply to oil exploration companies in Pakistan, but here too domestic demand was limited. In 1991, shortly after moving to Islamabad, I founded Zaver Petroleum Corporation, named after my beloved mother, and entered into a JV with the Oil and Gas Development Authority of Pakistan.

The Hashoo Group had a 10 per cent stake in the JV and we began to explore several fields. We were successful with Chanda, near Kohat in northern Pakistan. It still produces oil. In 1995, Occidental Petroleum's Pakistan subsidiary was put on sale by its American owners. Its oilfields were depleting and the management did not want to invest in further exploration. I bought Occidental Petroleum Pakistan and brought it under the Zaver Petroleum umbrella. Through that company we applied for new blocks and also renewed the exploration of existing and supposedly depleted fields in Sindh and northern Punjab (in Pothwar, near Islamabad). This acquisition also gave us access to a gas block in Balochistan. I had great hopes when I bought Occidental Petroleum Pakistan and wanted to expand and scale up. One of the routes was to make further acquisitions. Burmah Oil, the Scottish energy giant, was ready to sell its controlling stake in Pakistan Petroleum Limited. In the mid-1990s, I signed an agreement with them and got the necessary clearances from the government. Then, in 1996, the government changed and President Farooq Leghari objected. Nawaz Sharif's second government went to court to block the transaction. It was happy to have Pakistan Petroleum and its assets owned by the Scottish but not by a Pakistani conglomerate.

Just before this, Occidental Petroleum Pakistan— renamed Orient Petroleum Inc. (OPI)—had won the rights to explore five additional blocks. Well after the bidding process had been concluded, the government played dirty. Anwar Saifullah Khan, minister for petroleum in Benazir's second administration—also the son-in-law of Ghulam Ishaq Khan—suddenly demanded a bank guarantee of 65 million dollars. This was unheard of. Where was the question of a hefty bank guarantee for merely oil exploration, without any asset having been discovered? I wrote to the government. Why was I being victimized as a Pakistani? After all, such last-minute changes in conditions would not have been resorted to in case of an international company. A few days later, I was called to a meeting by Zardari. To my surprise, Anwar Saifullah was already in the room. The minister told me to surrender one block from the five allotted to me. They wanted to give it to a Polish company, even though the bidding period was over. I realized this was one of Saifullah's little side ventures and shrugged my shoulders: 'Take it if you want.' Even after that, the bank guarantee clause was not removed. Finally, I furnished the guarantee but, by then, the government had been dismissed. Chaudhary Nisar Ali Khan, who came in as Nawaz Sharif's petroleum minister in 1997, sought to cancel the allotment of the four remaining blocks. I went to court and finally Nisar Ali Khan called a meeting to reach a compromise. The formula he offered entailed surrender of two more blocks in favour of the government, which would be given to the state-run Oil and Gas Development Authority. I agreed, for I was left with no choice. Even if with only two blocks, I needed to start work. I had hired international technicians for the exploration and was paying them salaries while keeping them idle. The government had one final condition. A sixth block, Mehar, was already in OPI's possession. Nisar Ali Khan asked me to give a majority stake in Mehar to Petronas, owned by the Malaysian government. He said this was part of a bilateral arrangement between Islamabad and Kuala Lumpur. I was forced to sell 75 per cent of the equity to Petronas.

I was extremely disheartened by the lack of transparency in Pakistan and by the absence of a clear-cut oil and gas exploration policy. International companies were favoured, local companies discriminated against. It was frustrating and I began looking overseas. We registered a new company, Osprey Petroleum, in Nevada, having already acquired maps and three-dimensional survey documents related to nine wells in the Gulf of Mexico, just off Texas. Here we made discoveries, produced oil and sold it to refineries. The Hashoo Group also bought a block in the Dushan fields in Kazakhstan. We gave operating rights to a Canadian entity, PetroKazakhstan, later taken over by China National Petroleum Corporation. Its successor company, PetroChina, is now our partner. The Hashoo

Group is surveying oil opportunities in Iraq and has drilled seven wells in Sudan, so far without success. Indonesia and the Philippines are new frontiers that we will go to in the coming years. Finally, of course, there is the hope that one day we will be able to systematically exploit and extract the oil and gas resources of Pakistan—in Sindh and Punjab and Balochistan. The presence of prodigious shale gas potential in Pakistan and the new advances in fracking (induced hydraulic fracturing) technology have got me excited.

~

My remaining years will be consumed by the oil and gas business—which I imagine will be the final line of business I will go into in a sizeable manner—and by the Hashoo Foundation. The Foundation is completely independent of the businesses of the Hashoo Group. I hope to continue to support its efforts to make deep social investments in health and education, agriculture and sustainable livelihoods, particularly in the rural areas of Pakistan. I am deploying more and more of my time in this direction. I have no personal ambitions. I am more than happy with what Allah has given me. I believe in destiny, and I know it is written that one day, a day I don't know and cannot foretell, I will go. My soul will leave for its eternal abode and will be

233

answerable to Allah. I will depart with my hands empty; there will be no money, no wealth, no material possessions, no children, no worldly associations and bonds to keep me company. This doesn't scare me. My faith has given me courage—to live life honestly and truthfully, on my terms and without fear. My faith has also given me courage to be unafraid of death.

My faith has given me one more attribute—abounding optimism in Pakistan's future. For all its problems, this is a country blessed by God. It has natural gifts—agricultural plenty, energy resources, minerals—that so many other countries would covet. Unfortunately, no government has thought of—or been allowed to think of—using these resources for the good of the economy and the prosperity of the common Pakistani in a sustained manner. Politicians have thought of the short term. Generals have thought of the US. Few have thought of, or thought for, Pakistan. Two wars in Afghanistan, a generation removed, have taken their toll on Pakistan.

In some aspects, our society can be divided into the pre-Zia and post-Zia phases. Zia-ul-Haq's military raj, from 1977 to 1988, changed us for the worse. We are still recovering from it. He involved us in superpower conflicts, claiming this was justified in the name of jihad and Islam. He encouraged the opening of extremist madrasas and the preaching of theories antithetical to the pluralism and open-mindedness of Islam, a religion of peace and love and forgiveness. He misused every tenet of Islam. Muslims have a system of charity called *zakat*—voluntary sharing of 2.5 per cent of one's income with the needy and the underprivileged. Zia made zakat mandatory and began deducting it from bank accounts. Worse, he began using zakat funds for political purposes. This was unheard of among devout Muslims. Along with his series of religious laws, he created a society that was concerned with the symbols and outer layers of Islam and not with its essence and its profound philosophy. Somewhere and somehow, we need to roll back that period, which we are still paying for. Somewhere and somehow, we need to undiscover Zia and Zia-ism—and rediscover Islam in all its breathless, boundless beauty.

Somewhere and somehow, we need to empower the good, common citizens of Pakistan, particularly our young men and women. Somewhere and somehow, we need to take the path to the economic rejuvenation of Pakistan. Somewhere and somehow, we need to do this and we will do it.

I have faith in my people.

I have faith in my Pakistan.

Above all, I have faith in Allah.

ACKNOWLEDGEMENTS

I specially thank my loving daughter Sarah who persuaded me to undertake this memoir, by writing which I have fulfilled her desire for the youth to benefit from my experience and life struggle.

I also give special thanks to Ashok Malik who has helped me compile this memoir. I must admit that in my lifetime I have never read a book. He has taken a lot of effort to help me complete this book, which is my first. I know there will be more to follow.

INDEX

Index

Index

Index